Mother in 1905,

LIFE OF THE

Rev. Mother Amadeus

of the Heart of Jesus

Foundress of the Ursuline Missions
of Montana and Alaska

SKETCH COMPILED FROM CONVENT ANNALS

BY AN URSULINE OF ALASKA

New York
THE PAULIST PRESS
120 West 60th Street
1923

NOTE—*If we have used expressions which show our admiration for a record that seems to attain unto sanctity, we do so with complete submission to the verdict of the Church's authority.*

4448

DEDICATION

With tender love for the Immaculate Mother of God whom she so earnestly strove to resemble, in honor of the four magnanimous Bishops, Rappe, Gilmour, Brondel and Crimont, three of whom preceded her into the Great Beyond, and who, shadows of the Father, made her wonders possible, with deep gratitude toward our many Benefactors and Friends, this life of Mother Amadeus is offered by

AN URSULINE of Alaska.

PREFACE

I AM glad indeed that a life of Reverend Mother Amadeus has been written. She was truly one of those rare characters who show how beautiful our human nature can be at its best, and whose lives make it very clear that not only is life worth living, but that it can accomplish marvelous things in spite of the handicaps under which it labors. It becomes easier to understand that something deathless in us, when we see human beings accomplish so much of good, making all around them feel the deeper meaning of life while they do it.

Professor Osler, the distinguished Professor of Medicine at Johns Hopkins, our leading teacher of medicine in this country for years, until the English succeeded in tempting him by the bait of the Regius Professorship at Oxford, recognized very well the place of such characters as Mother Amadeus, not only in life, but in influencing the deepest thought of mankind. Asked to deliver the Ingersoll lecture on Science and Immortality at Harvard, he divided those who take the idea of Immortality seriously into three classes. The first class is the Laodiceans who announce that they believe in immortality, but who do not permit the idea to influence in any way their life here below. They are neither hot nor cold but lukewarm—of them we know what was said. The second class is the Gallionians, that is the conscious or unconscious followers of Gallio, the Roman Proconsul, who when the Jews haled St. Paul before him at Corinth said: "If it were of some matter of injustice I should with reason bear with you,

but if they be questions of words and names and of
your law, look you to it; I will not be judge of such
things." The Gallionians represent those who refuse
to think that religion can mean anything. They de-
liberately put the matter aside as one about which we
know nothing and have no means of knowing anything.

The third class Dr. Osler called the Teresians, the
conscious or unconscious disciples of that Teresa of
the Flaming Heart, for whom eternity meant so much
that her influence with regard to it touched all those
about her. She lived her life 400 years ago behind the
convent grill of Carmel in Spain, and yet editions of
her works are being issued in practically every cul-
tural language at the present time, and Spain celebrated
last year the three hundredth anniversary of her canonization with an outburst of praise and profound reverence seldom accorded to anyone and probably never
before to a woman. Osler spoke of the "serene faith
of Socrates with a cup of hemlock at his lips, the heroic
devotion of a St. Francis or a St. Teresa, but more often
for each one of us the beautiful life of some good woman whose

> 'Eyes are homes of silent prayer
> ....
> Whose loves in higher love endure.'

do more to keep alive among us a belief in immortality
than all the preaching in the land."

To my mind this is the sort of influence that Mother
Amadeus had. A delegate from Chili, in attendance
at the Pan-American conference of women in Washington, asked the National League of Women Voters
to select the names of twelve American women who

have done such good work in the United States that they deserve to be looked upon as models for the rising generation to know. She wished to write articles on them for the Chilean press. The League of Women Voters asked for help in answering the question, and I suggested six great American women who have accomplished wonderful work in America, beginning with Mother Seton, ending with Mother Alphonsa Hawthorne-Lathrop, and among them not the least was Mother Amadeus.

I then ventured to say of her:

> "With a group of Ursuline Sisters, she dared the bitter cold of the Farthest North of the United States, and faced the trials of life along with the Eskimo natives of Alaska, and succeeded in doing a deal of good for these people to whom civilization was only bringing its ills, not its benefits. The example of Mother Amadeus and her Sisters did more than anything else to tinge with a beauty of unselfishness and idealism and with a glow of thoughtfulness for others, the sordid incidents connected with the mad gold-rush to Alaska. Mother Amadeus was one of those wonderful souls who lifted up everybody that she came in contact with, and by her example taught those around her the lesson of immortality better than any amount of reasoning about it."

It has been said that St. Teresa kept back the tide of the Reformation in Spain and thus saved her country from the awful religious dissension which disturbed so many of the other countries of Western Europe, particularly during the sixteenth century. Possibly some might say that it was unfortunate that she did, since, had the Reformation come to Spain even with the attendant social disorders which so seriously rent

Germany and France and England, the Spaniards
would have been wakened from the lethargy into which
they were drifting and which has left their nation back-
ward in modern progress. Those who talk thus, however, have no proper notion of the history of Spain.
From shortly before Teresa's death until about a century after it, that is until the death of Calderon in 1681,
Spain was the artistic and intellectual leader in Europe,
and thereby of Western civilization. The great artists
Ribera, Velasquez, Murillo and many others of lesser
fame, the great writers Cervantes (who wrote what
Macaulay declared incomparably the best novel ever
written), Calderon, the only modern playright who
deserves to be compared with Shakespeare, as James
Russell Lowell thought, Lope de Vega most productive of novelists, Alarcon and the great spiritual writers,
as well as the makers of the wonderful Spanish arts
and crafts of the sixteenth and seventeenth centuries,
all did their work at this time.

Teresa from behind her convent grill, holding back
the tide of the Reformation, secured the peace for her
fellow countrymen which enabled them to accomplish
this great work. It is a never ending source of surprise
how the spiritual minded can thus deeply influence
their generation, though as a rule men refuse to believe such influence to be more than passing. Practical
minded people who pride themselves on their prac-
ticalness, are quite sure that it is only practical people
who do things that endure, but John Boyle O'Reilly
reminded us years before his own death,

> "The dreamer lives forever,
> And the toiler dies in a day."

If it is dreaming to make life's meaning all for eternity,

it is, indeed, a divine dream and that sort of dreamer Mother Amadeus was. Her memory will last when that of many who made their fortunes in the gold rush will have been long forgotten. She gathered a string of pearls, precious virtues, that are destined to influence deeply our American life for long years to come.

For this reason I deem it extremely important that her life should be written and if possible widely known. All those who came in contact with her during life, were deeply influenced by her. That influence can be extended by the written word to many, many more. Some would have us believe that the hand of the Lord is shortened, and that our generation has not been blessed by saintly persons as were the older days. I am not of those who so believe. For I have known some saints, and some of them are still with us. In recent years psychologists have suggested that reading the Lives of the Saints makes a very good discipline of mind for young people. Curiously enough this advice has come from those, very often, who were not themselves Catholics. The lives of our Catholic saints have been particularly recommended, and it has been suggested that we do not appreciate them at their full value until those outside the Church bring them to our notice in some special fashion.

Let us not fall under the blame of neglecting to appreciate fully the significance of the marvelously holy lives of some of those who were near and dear to us. Therefore it is that I welcome very heartily a life of Mother Amadeus of the Heart of Jesus, and wish for it that success and wide reading which I know it will deserve.   J. J. WALSH, M.D.

CONTENTS

CHAPTER I

Life of the Rev. Mother Amadeus

CHAPTER I

ANTECEDENTS

BEHIND every great influence exerted in the world, there is a long and most interesting history of contributing circumstances. Generally this history is untraceable, but one great charm attending historical studies in Amerca is that they concern events occurring in a world comparatively new, and their history can often be traced with more or less distinctness.

When England began making grants for Colonies in North America, the great size of the continent was unknown, and so, in a general way, the grants were understood to front on the Atlantic Ocean and extend to the Mississippi River. The first area definitely occupied by any particular colony took such shape as the colony was able to occupy consistent with the previous occupation of its neighbors, but always with the understanding that the colony had an interest in the great area west of the Alleghany mountains.

Shortly after the independence of the United States was recognized (1780-1785), this matter was settled by all the States deeding their interest in these lands to the General Government, except Connecticut. She retained 3,250,000 acres "on the southern shore of Lake Erie, which she wished to reserve for educational purposes.

This part of the State of Ohio is still commonly spoken of as the Connecticut reserve."

Of those fine lands, half a million acres were given to citizens of Connecticut whose property had been destroyed in the British raids upon the coast towns, and the rest were sold in 1795 for $1,200,000 "in aid of schools and colleges." [1]

The inhabitants of the six New England States were called "Yankees," and were reputed to be the shrewdest of all the American colonists. Of all these Yankees, those of Connecticut were considered the smartest, so that the phrase, "slick as a Connecticut Yankee," was supposed to represent the maximum of human intelligence. Now this Western Reserve, comprising a fifty-mile strip in the northeastern corner of the State of Ohio, along the southern shore of Lake Erie, was a rich and beautiful country of high, rolling land, traversed with many sparkling streams, producing great crops of corn, wheat, rye, oats, barley, all kinds of root crops, with great quantities of grapes. It had extensive deposits of potters' clay, many seams of bituminous coal and beds of iron ore, and not the least element of natural wealth was the great forests of oak, hickory, maple, cherry, and other hard woods.

Owing to its hilly character and numerous streams, it had abundant water power, and so furnished cheap, and almost unlimited, power for woolen mills, flour mills, and all kinds of manufactories. It was an ideal place for building up a rich and thriving settlement in the hands of an enterprising people capable of comprehending its advantages and energetic enough to profit by them.

1 Fiske, *Critical Period of American History*, p. 194.

This whole region was reserved by Congress for the people of the State of Connecticut. In the beginning it was settled and occupied almost exclusively by the most enterprising and intelligent people of that State, because the colonizing of the reservation was not done under Government patronage, but was in each case left to individual enterprise and exertion, and the "slick Connecticut Yankees" were not slow to avail themselves of the great advantages of this new promised land. Within less than half a dozen years they had spread themselves over all its broad expanse.

They had occupied all of the land, but only in a way. Each one had taken up all he could pay for with a view to selling a portion of it later.

The newcomers were not all farmers, but were from all grades of society, craftsmen of every kind, together with lawyers, doctors, merchants, preachers, teachers, speculators, and not a few capitalists, all on the lookout to make a fortune in this new country just opened for settlement. Teachers in particular were looking for engagements. The great educational fund provided by the sale of the lands insured an abundance of good schools. The people also levied a general tax for educational purposes, and the Western Reserve soon became celebrated as a great educational centre. Newspapers were established everywhere. Every man was a politician, and debating clubs and literary societies flourished. They were a very religious people, too, in their own way, everyone belonging to some church, and being very strict in attendance. It was a most lively, active community, a very hive of industry, and the whole settlement a scene of great intellectual activity. The dullest intellect reared in such surroundings must have been sharpened, a naturally bright one could hardly escape being polished to brilliancy. Only one thing was lacking. The Catholic Church had not been represented at all in the early settlement of the place, and it was not until many years after that even a few faint gleams of the true faith began to illumine the land.

To most of our western country, these gleams came with the advancing tide of settlements, first from France, by the way of New Orleans and St. Louis, and from Canada by the way of Quebec and Detroit. The fierce intolerance of the Puritans of the Western Reserve made the region so inhospitable to the volatile early French hunters and trappers, that the latter somewhat carefully avoided the Reserve. The first Catholic influence felt in this Puritan paradise came from Ireland. It is true that the first Catholic Bishop resident in the Reserve was a Frenchman, the saintly Bishop Rappe, but parishes precede Bishoprics, Missions precede parishes, and individual settlements must exist before mission houses can be established.

In the part of the Reserve where Mother Amadeus lived, the first "Mission House" or "Station" was the home of her family, the Dunnes or O'Dunnes of Iregan.

In early days in Europe, each region of country was governed by its own particular governing family, sometimes called tribe. Tribe was a larger term than family. The tribe governed the particular region, generally corresponding somewhat in area and jurisdiction with a county in the United States, and that area was called a "Country," and the chief of the tribe was called the "Prince" of that country and was the head of

that family. There were 180 such governing families
in Ireland, under the ancient Irish régime. The country
was divided nto four provinces, giving about 45 families
to each Province or Kingdom. Iregan, the country of the
O'Dunnes, was in Leinster. O'Dunne meant "of Donn,"
the eldest son of Milesius, who was drowned. From "the
Ogygie," an old Irish poem, we learn that Arech,
brother of Donn, went to Cualan, in Leinster, taking with him the children of Donn, and that a great chief
developed there called Donn Desa, from whom descended
Cahir Mor, Monarch of Ireland in the second century.
From him come the chief Catholic families of Leinster,
among whom the O'Dunnes were recognized as Princes
of Iregan until the time of Teige Reagh O'Dunne, the
last recognized Prince, in the time of James I.

Under the Elizabethan persecutions, a law was enacted that if a younger son of a Catholic family would
turn Protestant, he could get his proportionate share of
the principality by patent from the English crown, and
the rest of the principality should be confiscated and
sold to English settlers.

Iregan was thus dismembered, the old hunting lodge
known as "the Brittas" was patented by Charles I. to a
younger son, Barnaby, and his descendants hold it to
this day. The perpetuation of that possession has
served one good purpose in preserving the history of
the family and keeping in remembrance the descent of
the elder branch.

Humphrey O'Dunne was Lt. Col. of Dillon's regiment
in the service of France, and commanded the regiment,
in behalf of American Independence, at the siege of
Savannah. He was afterwards made Envoy Extraor-
dinary from France to the Court of Lisbon (in Por-

tugal). The great Irish scholar, O'Donovan, translator
of the Four Masters in 1830, found living on his farm
in Iregan the lineal descendant of Tiege Reagh O'Dunne,
recognized as such by the common tradition of the people. He died in 1840 without surviving heir. A few
years later another search was made by local anti-
quarians, and they found that the next heir was John
O'Dunne, who sailed for America in 1820 and settled in
the Western Reserve, in Northern Ohio, in 1836.

He was a youth of only twenty years when he set
out. He landed in upper Canada, where he bought a
tract of land, intending to found upon it a Catholic colony from Ireland, but finding too much opposition from
Orangemen there, he sold out and moved over to the
United States, where he engaged in railroad building
and other public works. After fourteen years of that
life he met, at Rochester, N. Y., another branch of the
O'Dunnes of Iregan, and married, in 1834, the youngest
daughter, Eleanor. They lived at Little Falls, Herkimer
County, N. Y., where their eldest child, Edmund, was
born.

This Little Falls was a beautiful town on the Mohawk
River, at the point where the river was crossed by the
great line of travel from the seaport city of New York
to the west. During the long, severe winters prevalent
at that place, outdoor public works were to a great extent suspended, and the contractors and operators were
housed, and passed the time talking about the most
likely place for operation during the coming summer or
for a permanent settlement on the land. Naturally, the
claims of the West were much discussed, and the delights of a settled life in a farming country, were con-
trasted with the aimless, roving life of a contractor on

public works. It is not surprising that the desire of the young wife and mother to have a settled home prevailed.

Then, as now, land speculators abounded in the West, and they were not slow to flood the East with pamphlets, maps, and circulars setting forth the attractions of their respective lands. Every hotel along the railroad, from Buffalo to Albany, was filled with them. The "slick Yankees" of the Western Reserve were not behind their neighbors in this respect, and so, when the time for travel came, in the spring of 1836, it found this little family of the O'Dunnes of Iregan on the way to the Western Reserve. The particular place they had in view was a thriving town, the county seat of a new county about forty miles south of the Lake, on the beautiful Cuyahoga River, and, as there was a cataract or "falls" in the river at this point, it was called Cuyahoga Falls.

Mr. O'Dunne looked about here for a little while and finally made a purchase of a block of city lots on the edge of the town, comprising in all a tract of a little over four acres, rather a large area of city blocks, but it was thought that, as the place was the county seat of a new and thriving county, the lots would rapidly advance in value and the investment prove very profitable. The original settler on this property had erected a neat log cabin on the corner of the land near the town. Mr. O'Dunne made some additions to this, and added a large frame building in which Mass was said by the first visiting priest, Rev. Father McLoughlin afterwards located, in 1852, at Brooklyn, New York. While these improvements were going on, the family boarded with a very nice Yankee family named Wilcox, living in a big, red frame house nearby, where was born the second child of this family, named Sarah. This bright, pretty child, a great favorite with the young ladies of the Wilcox family, died in her second summer.

The third child, John Joseph, was born in the spring of 1839. The next year, 1840, was a critical one in the history of this family. Up to this time, the head of the house had apparently been taking life very easily since the time of his marriage. He had been making a great change in his life. For fourteen years, he had led the busy, rushing, bustling life of a Government contractor on public works, principally in contracts for preparing the roadbed for railroads, including the stone work for culverts and bridges. These contracts being let to the lowest responsible bidder, involved great competition and necessarily much close calculation. Each contract was for preparing the roadbed for one or more miles in length, and the cost might vary from five thousand to fifty thousand dollars a mile, according to circumstances, and the amount of solid rock that would have to be cut through. To undertake such a contract, was like undertaking a military campaign. First, the line of road had to be cut through the giant forest, one or more hundred feet in width; then a removal from this path of the trunks of almost innumerable trees; then the digging out and removal of all the stumps, then the building in solid, massive rock of the culverts and bridges needed for drainage and the crossing of streams; lastly, the grading of the roadbed. All of this required a small army of men and horses with tools and equipments, and the building of houses all along the line for the accommodation of the workmen. As all the work was done by contract, it had to be done at a profit or not at all, so you may imagine everything was carried on at high pressure and rushed to the last possible degree. For fourteen of the best years of his life Mr. O'Dunne had lived at this high pressure. Now, for some years, he had been, as it were, resting and indulging in the most fascinating of occupations, the building up of a suburban home with a new house and grounds, with fruits, flowers, gardens, fields, and the thousand and one little things a young and loving couple find to ornament the home.

The savings of many years had been lavished with prodigal hands upon this delightful little property, when all at once, like a fire bell in the night, a note of alarm was sounded, and all the beauty of this fairy-like scene began to fade away. The fixing of the county seat at this place had been subject to a confirming vote to be taken later. It had been so taken for granted that this place would be confirmed as the permanent capital of the county that no other result was deemed possible, but when the votes were counted a new place called Akron, some miles away, had a majority of the votes, and in the expressive phrase of the country, "the bottom fell out of the town of Cuyahoga Falls." Practically, the great town lot property, corner lots and all, was blotted out from the map, and there remained only a large blank space which might be marked "O'Dunne's Land," useful for farming purposes, or, as viewed by the proprietor, of no particular use at present.

It was a great blow to the hopes of this family. Much of the savings of many years had been swallowed up in the long stay of over a year at Little Falls, in New York State, the romantic little village in the celebrated "Mohawk Vale." Then there were the successive drafts on the little capital for the great expense of the long journey out west, the purchase of the much vaunted, now nearly worthless suburban, town-lot property, including the cost of the ambitious, new, frame building, the new, handsome house in which the missionary Masses were celebrated. It was now like fairy money turned to paper, or like dead sea fruit, to ashes on the lips. Only those who have experienced such a bitter disappointment can realize its paralyzing effect; how all hope seems to die, until, after a while, new hopes spring up again.

What has all this to do with the life of Mother Amadeus? Everything. The best history of a life is the setting forth of the incidents which go to form the character of the person. A most potent influence in forming that character is the character of the mother. Character is formed mainly through suffering. The first great grief of the mother of Mother Amadeus was the loss of her infant daughter, Sarah. Death has always a sobering influence. The young mother who buries her first-born acquires a seriousness of manner which is never wholly lost. Life is never exactly the same to her again, and if, in addition to this, there come other troubles, the effect is often very great.

The underlying element which "made the place" at Cuyahoga Falls, the county seat location, being removed, it had no longer any attraction for the head of this family as a place of residence. Nearly everything had been removed to "Akron," the new county seat, and it seemed as if the only thing for this family to do was to move there also, but Mr. O'Dunne had never been much in the habit of yielding to the will of others. He was very much disposed to choose his own surroundings. When his father died in Ireland, in 1820, and left him alone, a youth of scarcely twenty years of age, he set out at once for America; when the Orangemen in upper Canada attempted to direct how he should control his land purchase, he sold his land and went to the United States. When circumstances seemed to conspire now to force him to move to Akron, he rebelled and determined to make a further exploration of this new western country, and so, straightening out his affairs as well as possible, and arranging for the comfort of his little family during his absence, he set out, on a prospecting trip, for the new city of Chicago. If only he had held to his first idea and remained there as one of the pioneers of the place, what a brilliant future he might have had. Chicago in 1840, and an energetic young man accustomed to handling large contracts in the way of building and improvements! What a combination! What a field of possibilities! Why did he not remain?

In whatever country a boy passes the play time of his youth, that remains for him, throughout all the years of his life, the most beautiful country in the world, and whatever country he looks upon in later years is attractive to him in proportion as it resembles or reminds him of the land of his youth.

Iregan, the ancient home of the O'Dunnes, was a mountain country traversed with sparkling streams. It was affectionately spoken of by its people as "The Mountain," and the war-cry of the tribe, as well as the motto of the family, was "Mullac a bu" or "The Mountain Forever!" The first twenty years of his life was passed by Mr. O'Dunne on his father's farm amid the green hills of Iregan.

His first choice of residence in America was in the highlands of upper Canada. His home in Little Falls

was in one of the most beautiful of mountain regions.
The Western Reserve in Ohio was a finely wooded country abounding in beautiful streams. His home town of
Cuyahoga Falls was an epitome of mountain scenery.
The low, flat country about Chicago was not inviting to
him. Moreover, the country was then intensely mala-
rious. For miles and miles along each side of the country roads he saw the fields shining with golden grain, and
not a soul to harvest it. The farmers were mostly sick
a-bed with malaria or chills and fever, as they variously
termed the prevailing ailment in all new countries where
low lying, rich land is first turned over and exposed
to the hot sun. The malaria of Illinois either killed
the early settlers outright or wrecked their constitutions
for life. Mr. O'Dunne fled the plague-stricken country
and hurried back to the health-giving hills of the Western Reserve, sold his town lots in Cuyahoga Falls, and
moved to the thriving town of Akron, the new county
seat of Summit County. The very names of the places
show the topography of the country, Akron, meaning
high, as in the Greek, Acropolis, the high city, and the
name Summit County shows that it was the highest land
in that region. A great canal had been built right
across the State, from the Ohio River on the south up
to the waters of Lake Erie on the north, with a branch
running from Akron to great coal and iron fields in
Pennsylvania on the east.

The carrying of a canal over the hills of Akron was
a triumph of engineering. In an incredibly short distance through the city of Akron, twenty-one locks were
required. This gave a great amount of water power,
and mills and factories abounded in the city, particularly flour and woolen mills, which greatly stim-

ulated wheat growing and sheep raising throughout the settlement. Everything conspired to make this town of Akron a busy hive of industry. Into this wonderful place came Mr. O'Dunne and his family, in the year 1842, the family having been increased by the birth, in 1841, of a daughter, Mary Ellen, subsequently in religion, Sister Mary of the Angels of the Ursuline Order. The family lived at first in a neat little frame house on Court Hill, in Akron, nearly east of the Baptist Meeting House. At this place, on the second of July, 1846, the bright little girl, Sarah Theresa, the subject of this memoir, was born.

CHAPTER II

CHILDHOOD

How attractive is the face of sanctity, as it smiles down upon these latter days.

It seems as though Grignon de Montfort's prophecy were on the eve of accomplishment, so many saints have recently appeared exercising untold magnetism and power: the world's Little Flower, Gabriel, the gracious Thaumaturgus of today, countless simple mystics who speak to us Our Lord's winning messages of love.

When we look at Mother Amadeus, we see all this, and yet there is, too, something of the Stylites about her, as she stands before us in gigantic forgetfulness of self, lifted high into God-all-aloneness, and yet drawing, drawing, souls, souls sunk in ignorance and degradation. Yet she smiles as she follows the beaten path of the Ursuline life, and charms us by her simplicity, her directness. She goes straight to the heart of her fellows, every one, as Abraham Lincoln did, and what Emerson said of him, we may say of her, her "heart was as great as the world, but there was no room in it to hold the memory of a wrong." The Cheyenne Indians do not say "I love you;" they have not the word. They say: "I take my heart and place it next to yours."

That was Sarah Theresa Dunne. We shall see.

Sarah Theresa Dunne was born on the Court House Hill, at Akron, Ohio, July 2, 1846. Her father, John Dunne, had come with the century on June 9th; her

14

mother, Ellen Dunne, of Pallace—though not related they bore the same name—ten years later, on May 1st.

They were married at Rochester, N. Y., on September 13, 1834.

Edmund, who lived to champion the Catholic schools and whose life must some day be written, was the first to rejoice the devoted pair. Then came the little Sarah, who soon left this earth, on June 5, 1838. John Joseph, Col. Dunne of Philadelphia, came next; then Mary Ellen, professed of Cleveland Ursuline Convent, where she died September 13, 1882, and then the subject of our sketch, to whom her loving parents gave the name they seemed particularly to cherish: Sarah, the Beautiful. Those to whom it was given to know Mother Amadeus intimately, see a fitness in this choice, as also in that of Theresa taken in Confirmation and Amadeus which her religious profession gave.

The home at Akron served as the church whenever Father McCann came around. This distinguished scholar from Maynooth loved the home of John and Mary Dunne, and as little Sarah grew old enough to attract his attention, he used to lift her up on his knee and talk to her about her First Communion. The future "Theresa of Alaska" understood, and when she was eight years old, Father McCann gave her Our Lord, and espoused them both, the Great Mighty One, the little pure one.

She wore a white dress on that sweet first of days, tiny patent leather shoes about which her brother, John, kept teasing her, and a wreath of honeysuckle. The little one attracted great attention that morning, for never in the fifties was a child so young admitted to the Sacred Banquet. But the scholar from Maynooth was ahead of his time, and Our Lord was preparing the soul of her who was to bring to Him the little ones of the Arctics. Father McCann enjoyed little Sarah's bright, pretty ways. Her father was the friend of all his fellow-countrymen; not one but turned to him for help and advice. One day, when her parents were out, tiny Sarah answered the door bell: "Please, Ma'm," dropping a courtesy and the richest brogue, "is this where the serviceable Irishman lives?" she was asked. She repeated the message later in all its local color, and her arch pretty way only enhanced the value of the compliment. This little girl clung to her mother but stood in awe of her stern father. She would watch her mother's eye, and catch from it the clue to how she should behave: "Now, chldren," the mother would often say, "keep still: do not worry your father," and Sarah would tiptoe away to play elsewhere, leading her older sister, Mary.

At that age she could already read aloud to the proud, fond father. A rigid disciplinarian was he, most exact, most eager for his children's improvement. Whenever business took him away from home, he would expect letters from the four little ones, and oh! beware the mistakes in spelling. Mr. Dunne would cut them out of the letters, and return them to the writer. Sarah, to whom this never happened, would stand on tiptoe when letters came "from father," and count the little slips of paper as they fell out of the letters of the others, but always with the ringing laugh, the kindly smile that took the edge off everything she did. Her brothers were so proud of her; they loved to accompany her to school, carrying her books. One day—this was the day of bigotry in the Western Reserve—the teacher under-

took to speak against the Church. Up rose Sarah, the
tiniest in the crowded schoolroom. "I am going home,"
she said. "My mother told me that I should not listen
to any lies against the true Church, for I am an Irish
Catholic." And gathering up her slate, her books,
Sarah was off before teacher and pupils recovered from
their astonishment. She was received in the open arms
of her noble mother, and as the two hearts throbbed in
unison, the older kept thinking: "What is to become
of this child? for surely the grace of God is with her."
When school was out, the principal appeared at the
Dunne residence, and the offense was not repeated, for
fear of the little daughter of the Kings of Iregan.

The second chapter of Sarah's life wore on, all
sunshine, all joy. Though she was so tiny, so delicate,
she stood in the sunshine of everyone's heart, this embryo foundress, laughing, leading, praying, playing.
Her brothers write of her: "She was our youngest, always considered pretty, very bright and active, good-
natured, keen, witty, courageous. Her eyes were steel
blue and very clear; her hair, golden at six, changed at
nine to light brown; her forehead, rounded and pro-
truding." The lines of the child's face mirrored her
character—there were no angles—all was winning,
sweet, attractive, sunny.

One day, when she and Mary walked home from
school, they were tempted by their companions into a
raspberry patch. They had strict orders to come right
home, and their consciences were troubling them as they
furtively gathered some of the forbidden fruit. "Oh!"
they thought, as they finally broke away from temptation, "if mother could only forget to look at the clock."
But mother had not forgotten. They beheld her sad-

dened, anxious countenance looking down the street, as they drew near, and oh! how they hated the raspberries.

"And now," said Mrs. Dunne, "I did not think *my* little girls would ever disobey me. I shall have to write to your father."

The little girls wept, and begged for any other punishment; they promised the fault would never be repeated if only she would not write it to "father." And as they lay in bed that night, the little sisters promised they would never, never again stop on their way home from school. They talked long of their mother; their father, whom they loved so well and yet so differently; of their dear brothers, John and Edmund; Edmund, the oldest, whom they had been taught to revere, and who had gone with their father to California. Soon mother and John would follow, and the little girls would be sent to the Convent boarding school.

Sarah was faithful to her good resolution, but Mary succumbed. Mrs. Dunne had a beautiful orchard, and she was raising peaches for the county fair. One was ripening—a very beauty—the certain prize winner, so she took her little girls out to see it, telling them not to pluck it, and why.

But Mary could not resist the pink cheek that caressed hers. She did not pluck the fruit, but she stood on tiptoe and took one delicious bite.

Sarah was scandalized, and said so to her sister. She stood trembling at the thought of her mother's disappointment. When questioned, she merely answered, "No," she had not done it, and then the dear mother was disarmed by Mary's frank avowal of her guilt.

Sarah was even then the leader, the heart winner.

But time was closing in about this sweet, sunny

RT. REV. AMADEUS RAPPE, FIRST BISHOP OF CLEVELAND.

childhood. Letters came from California saying that
Edmond, though only sixteen, had made his mark in the
West and that the father was settled in his new home
anxious for his wife, whom John should bring out to
him. Mrs. Dunne was not well, and all thought that
the Pacific Coast would benefit her. Often did little
Sarah steal to her mother's bedside and pour out upon
her the treasures of her deep, loving heart in her own
little silent way, so tender, because so sincere and true.
How many were the ministrations of that little hand:
Though Mrs. Dunne had a very skillful cook who knew
also the womanly art of nursing, Sarah resented it, and
went away sad when she was removed from her
mother's bedside and Mrs. B.'s offices were substituted.

Two years had sped away since her First Communion, she was ten years old now, and must be off to boarding school with Mary.

The little girls had always been most carefully, most
beautifully dressed by their fond mother; they had been
trained to scrupulous order and cleanliness, and all they
had was unsurpassed.

The dear mother began packing their trunk for
boarding school, and a mother-packed trunk is a poem
—a history of the past, a protecting prayer for the future. All these little things had a voice, repeating
mother's teachings and hoping the separation would not
be long.

Sarah was never to see her mother again. Mrs.
Dunne tenderly gave her daughters into the hands of her
dear son, John, while her heart told her she was laying
a costly sacrifice upon the altar of God.

CHAPTER III

Boarding School

THE old Ursuline Order, the first founded in God's Church for the education of young girls, had from the very beginning taken deep root in France.

In 1535, St. Angela Merici had founded it at Brescia upon the model of a vision vouchsafed her at the vintage of Brudazzo. She had seen angels ascending to Heaven upon a mysterious ladder leading maidens, wonderful maidens, each bearing on her brow a glistening gem, symbolic of learning and purity, those twin-born sisters of the Kingdom of God, and a voice said to the Saint: "Thou shalt not die till thou found at Berscia a company of virgins similar to these." It was told her, too, that her Order should never perish from the Church, and that it would be mighty to stem the tide of irreligion, then just beginning to show a menacing head. God works slowly, but when He does begin, we find the way prepared for a glorious success.

This tiny seed, cast by angel hands into the heart of their earth-born sister, Angela, took root not only in Italy, but almost simultaneously in France, then in Germany, England, and throughout Europe. Groups of educators sprang up around it who sought, through pontiff and prelate, a place 'neath the banner that the humble Angela had placed in Ursula's hand. Ursula, the leader by excellence, was patroness of learning in those days; universities sought her protection and kept her feast, and art found in her story its highest ideal.

St. Angela was not therefore guided by her humility alone when she chose the name of her "Company" of educators. Her lofty ideal was further emphasized when she placed her Virgins also beneath the protection of another woman, noted for purity and learning, St. Catherine of Alexandria, the philosopher, the martyr.

And God blessed, and still continues to bless, the virgin-born seed.

One of the most noted of these Ursuline Convents was that of Boulogne-sur-mer. Standing almost within sight of the chalk-cliffs of Albion, it had attracted many pupils from the heresy-torn land beyond the Channel. Boulogne had opened wide its heart and stretched wide its buildings, and gathered in many of St. Angela's industrious bees, to flit about in the garden of youth, gathering honey for the Lord.

One of the most distinguished Superiors of the monastery, Mère St. Maxime, had re-opened it after the storm of the French Revolution had blown over the land, and laid low the stately oak of Ursuline education. But "monks and oaks are eternal," and so the great oak began again to spread out its branches, and to shelter the birds of God's air, the dear blessed children.

One of the humbler workers in the convent, in its early restoration period, when a child, was gathering strawberries in her neighbor's patch on her way to school one morning, when the saintly mendicant, St. Benedict Joseph Labré, passed along the highway, and rebuked her for what he knew, by inspiration, to be theft. Three other distinguished ladies were making their novitiate in that blessed school of Ursuline sanctity, Sister Julia Chatfield, a convert, daughter of the Lord Mayor of London, Sister Annunciation, Sister Sacred

Heart—three so closely united, then, who were to spread afar into distant lands the resistless radiance of their loveliness.

Mother Sacred Heart died at the age of eighty-two, having been twenty-one years Mistress of Novices, and twenty-four years Superior at Boulogne, one of the most efficient Superiors the convent had ever known.

As usual, God's dear Providence was watching and working from afar. The Convents of France are singularly blest in their chaplains, the post of chaplain of the Ursulines being coveted by the most learned and pious priests. Nor was Boulogne an exception, for here labored Father Rappe, the golden hearted, who hid the fire of missionary zeal beneath his books and educational labors. He was very busy studying and praying one day, when another "John the Baptist from the Wilderness" knocked at his door. No less a man was this than the great John Baptist Purcell, Archbishop of Cincinnati, the pioneer Churchman of the West. He was in quest of missionary priests—he was in quest of Ursulines, and he captured Father Rappe and Mother Julia Chatfield, the freshly-professed novice.

And here begins the lovely Odysseus of the Ursuline Order, God's sweet epic. Three nuns from Boulogne, headed by Mother Julia Chatfield, and four from Beaulieu under the leadership of Mother St. Stanislaus Laurier, sailed to the United States, and opened at St. Martin, Brown County, Ohio, one of the most wonderful convents the Order has known.

"Noter Mère," as the Superor was fondly called, had not long been settled in her new home when, in 1850, she heard that Father Rappe had gone back to France and brought her dear sister novice, Mother Annuncia-

tion, back to open an Ursuline Convent in Cleveland, of which city he himself had been consecrated first Bishop.

The co-foundresses with Mother Annunciation were Mother Charles, Mother Seraphine, dear "Ma Sœur Bénoit," and Miss Arabella Seymour, a lady of rank and fortune, who followed the missionaries from the "Alma Mater," and later gave her talents and her worldly goods to the Order, as the beloved Mother Austin.

It was on July 20th of the year 1850 that the brave colony set sail from Havre to reach New York August 5th, and Cleveland two days later. On August 6th, they had their first Mass on Miss Arabella's trunk, transformed into an altar. On the feast of the Assumption, Our Lord, in His sacramental presence, took up His abode in their midst. And when that happens, an Ursuline Convent may be said to be founded. Mother Julia Chatfield came from Brown County to bid her sister novices welcome to the missionary field. These journeys are nothing now, but then, in the days of strict enclosure, of grind, of poverty, of the unknown, they remind us of one who "went in haste" to minister in the hilly country.

It is the meeting of the Ursuline Paul and Anthony in the desert. And at the side of each of these great pioneer women stood a great pioneer bishop, Bishop Purcell, Bishop Rappe.

We can scarcely translate into words the poetry and the perfume of these early days, so big with possibilities, for every child that knocks at the door of an Ursuline Convent may be another Theresa, "A Theresa of the Arctics." And that is what stepped into the maternal fastness of the arms and the heart of Mother Annunciation of Cleveland with Sarah Theresa Dunne in the year of Our Lord, 1856.

Contact with these great souls, Bishop Rappe and Mother Annunciation, helped to mold the little girl's character to heroism. They loved the child from the very first, so bright, so beautiful, so winning was she. Her delicate frame Mother Annunciation cared for with the delicacy of mother love, nurtured in the Ursuline heart. In the Ursuline Convent, Sarah, "The Beautiful," met many friends. First came Bishop Rappe, then her Ursuline Mothers, types to her ever afterwards of perfect womanliness. Then there were her classmates: Mother Ligouri, afterwards Superior of the "Alma Mater," and Mary and Josie Warner, daughters of Colonel Francis Warner of Vicksburg, Miss., with whom she formed one of those strong friendships of which we scarcely read save in the story of God's saints.

One day the games were at their height, and Sarah, as usual, the leader in the race, was running at top speed, when she spied Mary Warner in a corner of the recreation grounds, weeping because of the temporary absence of her sister, Josie. Sarah at once broke loose from the race and, nestling close to the little weeper, she said: "What is the matter with you, Mary. I have never seen you cry before, and even now there is salt in your tears." So Mary explained that she was lonesome for Josie, and with these simple words began the poetry of a friendship that lasted for sixty years without rupture or fever heat. Mary and Sarah were henceforth inseparable, and the former, now a nun at the Ursuline Convent of Toledo, Ohio, declares that: "Not once have I seen the least disrespect toward any nun in their respective charges or demands. Sarah never

showed impatience or reserve to any student in the
building under any circumstances she may have had to
confront. Never was she rude or rough in look, word, or
act, though we were many and of different temperaments.
In school, no one could surpass Sarah in class standing,
so bright was she. Sarah would divest herself of everything to give pleasure to another. I never knew her to
make an unkind remark of any human being, and this
feature alone would mark her as one of God's darlings.
Self-sacrifice was the leaven of her life, and with her
characteristic spiritual make-up, was it a wonder that,
later in life, she undertook things so great for God in
the West and in the North."

Little Sarah would often stop in the midst of her
play and say to her companions: "Some day I shall be
a missionary in the Rocky Mountains and in Alaska."
And the astonished girls would answer: "Oh! Sarah,
you won't either, you know you won't." "You will all
see," little Sarah would answer, and then on with the
game, with that energy and wholesouledness that afterwards founded the Missions of Montana and Alaska.

A programme for the distribution of prizes at the
Ursuline Convent of Cleveland, July 30, 1857, awards
to Sarah Dunne, a year after she had entered
school, the "crown of good behavior and religious
instruction in the Junior Class, an *"accessit"* in reading,
writing, grammar, orthography, and a premium in history, geography, and arithmetic." And, on another programme, dated July 22, 1858, her name appears in
the third division of the Senior Class for an *"accessit"*
in application and premiums in grammar, history, arithmetic, and bookkeeping.

Whilst she was studying, she was praying and

playing, this future missionary, and beginning that life
of heroic penance and self-crucifixion that she practised till death. Her beautiful body was her slave, delicate though it was, it had nothing to say. It was only
the alabaster vase, through which shone the radiant
soul, like a light within. Had it not been for the wise
maternal care of the Ursulnes of Cleveland, the
little one would have gone to Heaven, her great work
undone. Simple, straight, direct, her senses keen and
penetrating, she stood like a fawn on the edge of the
dark forest of life with the sunshine of the love of
everyone playing about her. The girls used to wonder
how she knew it, but she always knew ahead of time
when she was to receive a letter from mother or father
or the two fine brothers in California. She would say
to her sister: "Mary, we have a letter in that pile of letters Sister is bringing in." "How do you know, Sarah?"
"Do you not smell the salt air?" And little Sarah was
always right. Letters then came around the Horn from
San Francisco to New York, and thence to Cleveland,
and it is possible that the little one's keen sensibilities
discovered traces of the long sea journey.

The parents wrote frequently; they were proud of
their children's progress, and though their hearts hun-
gered for them, they felt so safe, so happy to know they
had left them in the care of the excellent Ursuline
training. John and Edmund were doing splendidly,
each making his mark and sending checks every month,
with directions to the nuns that Mary and Sarah should
have all they wanted.

Sarah used to spend many hours on her knees, erect
and without support, before the Most Blessed Sacrament
when It was exposed. She thought the Ostensorium

was the most beautiful thing she had ever seen, and
she listened, wrapt, to the voice of the Divine Artificer
who was molding her soul from afar, silently, irresist-
ibly, as is His wont.

In 1859, Father Gaudentius, C.P., came to Cleveland
to preach the children's annual retreat. This gentle
ascetic was one of the founders of the austere Order of
the Passionists in the United States, friend of the distinguished Father Dominick of the Mother of God who
received Cardinal Newman into the Church.

Contemplation of the sufferings of Christ Our Lord
seems to breed wonderful sanctities in this Order, an
attractive and irresistible sweetness and power which
find its culmination now in the magnetic boy, St. Gabriel
of Our Lady of Sorrows. At every page of their chronicle, we read wonderful names in the Order of the Passion. As the lightning leaps from peak to peak, the love
of the Most Blessed Sacrament spread its radiance about
the little girl who so often knelt there. Father Gaudentius noticed Sarah. He called her to the foot of Our
Lady's statue before the close of the retreat, and there
allowed her to consecrate herself to God by the irrev-
ocable Vow of Chastity.

I have never seen a sweeter scene than this one as
my mind sees it now. The beautiful child whose simple
white dress could not be so dazzling as the purity it
typified, her bright starlike eyes kept the simplicity
of the child even when they had put on the dignity of
womanhood, the lips so firm in their answer, their
prayer, the expression of the heaven-born desire, unwavering in their immolation, the old man worn with
austerity and labors, the angels and their Queen looking
down. It was on the eleventh of July. And when it

was over, the old Passionist could not help saying to Mother Annunciation: "This child looks like the little Mary in the Temple."

Up to the very last July 11th of her blessed life, July 11, 1919, Mother Amadeus always kept the day in silent, wondering gratitude. And the look of her eye, both magnetic and childlike, remained, and the last act of her life was to raise those eyes with a look of joyous and triumphant recognition of Someone. Was it the Queen to whom she had pledged herself on July 11, 1859? Sweet school days sped on to graduation, and the girls began to talk, as girls will talk, about the future.

CHAPTER IV

The Parting of the Ways

The Two Little Girls Enter the Novitiate

Soon came a letter from California. It was a letter from John. The children had not mentioned their vocations in their weekly letter home, so their brother wrote that he would soon come on to bring them to California. With characteristic directness and power, Sarah answered for both: she and Mary had decided to become Ursulines. The loving brother answered in turn that one might remain, but that the other must come out to the home in the Golden State. Let them decide which one it would be. Again Sarah answered for both: "We have the right to frame our own future. But if you insist, we shall both come, and if our lives prove unhappy, the blame will be on you." And thus the grave matter was decided.

The stanch Catholics, Mr. and Mrs. Dunne, were only too happy to have their daughters brides of Heaven, and by return mail sent their blessing and the desired consent.

Sarah Theresa hesitated not to break the golden link which bound her to father and mother and tenderly beloved brothers. With the same unwavering generosity, she snapped the still tenderer chord that bound her to Mary. They had never been separated, not even for a day, and now Sarah arose, and when Mary said she would enter the Novitiate in Cleveland, she answered unflinchingly: "And I am going to Toledo." Her soul had been the mistress always, and now her constant practice of cheerful self-denial budded this beautiful flower of detachment.

How truly wonderful the young girl who stands "where brook and river meet," who breaks away from the past, and plunges trustfully into the future, leaning upon the arm of the Beloved "crucified nineteen hundred years ago." He has never been known to deceive, or abandon, and when the snows of age and sorrow fell over the *"Sposina"* of that day, she found Him at her side, as in the days of her youth, so loving, so unchanged, so true.

On the twelfth of December, just four days after the great proclamation of 1854, the Cleveland community had opened a house in the rising city of Toledo.

Mother des Séraphins, an Ursuline of contemplative mold, professed of Boulogne, one of the original band, was sent to open the house on the Maumee. With her went Mother Alphonsus, the beloved mistress of the boarders, the energetic teacher and business woman of Cleveland. Though tried as are all foundations, this one quickly took root, and when, in 1861, Sarah Theresa Dunne knocked at the door, she found Mother Alphonsus in charge and the community numbering seven. Mother des Séraphins had returned to Boulogne, where she died November 11, 1880. Her memory has survived clad in the halo of the contemplative, weaving and working in silence and prayer the beautiful design of the Ursuline interior life, amid the charms of distinction and leisurely elegance of manner.

But Mother Alphonsus rises before us like the Ursuline "that does things," the giant ready to win in the race, in whom the strong hidden interior spirit buds the fruits of vigor and energy.

"With the fruit of her hands she hath planted a vineyard. She hath opened her hand to the needy, and stretched out her hand to the poor." God seems to have chosen these two women to be the Mary and Martha of the new house, especially for laying deep and strong and true the structure where the foundress of the missions of Montana and Alaska was to have her religious formation. Mother Alphonsus, a pupil of the Ursulines of Brown County, was a most noble Ursuline, a rigid observer of Poverty and the Rule, standing for regular observance, such as stand in the van of the armies of Israel, and plant there the tents of religious life. She was gifted also with that magnetism necessary to attract and hold ardent, generous youth in the paths of renunciation. Bishop Rappe was her adviser and helper, and he, too, smiled when he saw his little Theresa standing on the threshold of Toledo Convent. Good stock is this; he had seen it in France. He knew the old Ursuline tree. He had helped to plant it in that paradise of peace, "Old Brown County." His first care, when consecrated Bishop, had been to secure an Ursuline Convent for Cleveland, nor had it long taken root when a branch must be culled from the parent stem for Toledo. For the holy Bishop knew and felt for his diocese what Louis Veuillot said of France: "If the women of France remained Catholic in the seventeenth century, we must thank the Ursulines."

And when Sarah Theresa Dunne, with the bloom of schoolroom youth and beauty fresh upon her cheek, stepped from the graduating halls of Cleveland into the Novitiate of Toledo, she found at her side Bishop Rappe,

the first of the four great bishop friends who made possible the wonders of her wonderful life. He knew her
parents well, he loved the little soul thus confided to his
care, and well did he prove this love.

Besides Mother Alphonsus, our postulant found in
Toledo Convent, Mother Immaculate Heart and two
other postulants, Sisters Joseph and Aloysius. When
she reached the convent, the energetic Superior met her
at the door; disguising her great joy, under an assumption of business preoccupation—Sarah had come osten-
sibly on a visit to recuperate after her hard study.
"Here child," said Mother Alphonsus, by way of greeting, "you are welcome. Take my black apron and go
teach my geometry class. I am busy." And off she
went to her office, singing in her jubilant heart: "My
successor is here."

Our little candidate for the religious life was delighted. She herself was so direct, so sincere. She
knew that an Ursuline's black apron is almost a part of
her habit, the insignia of her sacred avocation. So off
she went to the classroom, which she left only a few
years later for the cell of the Superior. She was, from
the very first day, the darling, the hope of the community. Her unruffled temper, her wonderful judgment,
her unvarying amiability, and deep-seated habit of penance and self-sacrifice, made so perfect a whole, and one
so magnetic, so truly Ursuline, that they could not help
hoping for the success of their beloved house. Bishop
Rappe was a frequent visitor, and he always wanted to
see *"Ma petite Thérèse"* when he came over from Cleveland.

The young teacher had often asked for the cap, but
she had been put off, again and again, on account of her

delicate health. At length dawned the feast of the Immaculate Conception in 1861. The feast had always been her favorite, and today Sarah Theresa's heart was full of the light and joy we all feel when we know God is on our side. She began early to beg Mother Alphonsus to give her the "cap," the first insignia that was to admit her into the Novitiate. Wearied by the resistless pleadings of the fervent petitioner and her own maternal heart, Mother Alphonsus at length said: "Well, child, go and ask the Bishop."

Off flew Sarah Theresa, on the wings of her strong will, to the episcopal residence. His Lordship was busy that afternoon, and still the Spouse-elect of Christ sat waiting in the parlor, waiting, undaunted, to see the Bishop, for the strong will always conquers.

At length, Bishop Rappe came in to her. He knew her well, he knew he was arguing in vain against that vocation of adament. He spoke, however, of her youth, her delicate health, her parents way off in California, her sister who had just then taken the coveted cap in Cleveland. And while they argued, the pure child and the kind theologian, the shadows of night had begun to wrap them round and the feast of the Immaculate Conception was waning for another twelvemonth. At length, the Bishop sent the triumphant child back to the convent under the protection of his housekeeper. She had his permission and blessing. She ran to Mother Alphonsus. "But, child," said the secretly delighted Mother, "the nuns have gone to bed." "Never mind, Mother, Call them up, I must be received tonight. It is the Feast of the Immaculate Conception." So up rose the professed nuns to see their darling take her first step in the religious life. With her cap, the young mathematician also received charge of the accounts of the house, and off she skipped to bed. To bed, but not to sleep—she was too happy for sleep; she kept jumping up and down during this the first night of her long and fruitful religious life, to try on her dear, dear cap, to hug it and to lay it reverently back upon its chair again. Then she would lie quiet, her blue eyes wide open, longing for the first call to morning meditation. She was wondering, in the delight of her heart, what her two sister postulants would think when, in the sacred silence of the morning hour, they saw her rise, don the new livery, follow them into the chapel, kiss the floor, and begin her morning meditation.

What spiritual ambitions! What love of our Lord was required to keep young lips silent when they were bursting to speak! "Mother" understood and mercifully granted them a little recreation at the end of the breakfast lest their joyful hearts should burst with what they had to say. They were so glad Sarah had the "cap" at last, they were going to be so wonderfully good, and one of them was right.

In mission countries, and in the blessed early days of every religious house, the letter of the Rule, though never its spirit, is often obliged to yield to necessity. Indeed, Our Lord seems to write the spirit all the deeper, truer, into the hearts of the generous obedient ones that gayly shoulder burdens heavier than the merciful Rule imposes.

And thus we find this the youngest child of the house embracing the arduous duties of Syndica and teacher. Nor was she ever absent one hour from her teacher's desk, not one moment late at the community observances. On Saturdays, after Mass, Mother Al-

Rt. Rev. R. Gilmour, Second Bishop of Cleveland.

phonsus sent her to bed that she might recuperate for the duties of the week, but Sister Dunne had her accounts, and kept busy even then. Her accounts were always perfect, a blot, an error, an erasure, were undreamed of.

One of the rules of the wise and vigorous Superior was that the nuns should eat all that was set before them, and every morning each found a crust of dry bread on her plate. They were very poor, the Civil War was on, the roughest cotton skirts and underclothing of flour sacking was all they could have. A few tears fell sometimes, but fastidious delicacy soon gave way before the inevitable, and what Mother Alphonsus called the great (O)bedience, and the young people soon began to taste the sweet fruits of Poverty and Penance in increased vigor, rosy cheeks, clear, bright eyes, strength for the classroom, and a good appetite for dinner.

Under the cover of an entrancing smile and the uniformity of the Common life, penance was steeling the strong, masculine soul of Sarah Theresa. Her will was growing stronger, her will absolutely fearless, because filled with unwavering trust in God. Daughter of the Kings of Iregan, she was daughter, too, of the virgins, the martyrs.

On September 2, 1862, the three happy, careless postulants, the first to be received in the Toledo Convent, were clothed in the dear old habit of the saints, Sarah Theresa receiving the name of Mary Amadeus, by which dear name shall we ever know her.

She was the pet of Bishop Rappe, hence she received his name, "Amadeus." The holy old man could not conceal his joy when he saw his child clothed in the

name and in the habit he loved so well. Forgetful of
the vile things of earth, as Our Lord with St. John, he
kissed the soul that shone out upon the maidenly brow:
"And now, I beseech thee, lady, not as writing a new
Commandment, but that which we have had from the
beginning, that we love one another." [1]

When souls, like Our Lord, go up into the mountain,
a cloud receives them out of our sight, peer through it
as we will. All we can gather of the Novitiate days of
our Sister Mary Amadeus, is that the one she so lovingly
called Mother, showed this brave young soul the religious life in its beautiful and winning austerity and
asceticism. For that alone could hold it and give that
ideal strength, that tender union with God implied in the
word "Ursuline." Who would leave the loves, the
blandishments of home, for a lax Novitiate? None, I
think, wittingly, and the souls that placed themselves
under Mother Alphonsus' direction, knew not this keen-
est of all disappointments.

When Reginald Pakenham, of "Her Majesty's Cold
Steam Guards," nephew of the great Wellington, gave
up his flattering worldly prospects and left Her Majesty's
ranks for those of Paul of the Cross, in the austere life
of the Passionists, the world was angered, amazed. All
the brilliant young officer's friends, save one, concluded
that study had injured his mind. But the grand old
Duke of Iron jumped into a cab, drove to the Novitiate,
and clapping his heavy hand on the novice's shoulder,
said: "My son, I understand you. Be a soldier here
as you were on the field, as obedient, as submissive to
discipline. Go through your Novitiate." Sister Amadeus "went through her Novitiate."

1 2 St. John v.

On August 23, 1864, Sister Mary Amadeus pro-
nounced her holy vows. Mother St. Mary, her former
teacher, then Superior in Cleveland Convent, came to
Toledo for the occasion, bringing with her the beloved
sister, Mary, the newly professed, who had but first
taken her vows, and who, as Sister Mary of the Angels,
was greatly beloved by the Cleveland house. The two
sisters had not met since they parted in the graduation
hall of Cleveland, Mary to enter there, and Sarah to set
her face toward Toledo. They loved each other most
tenderly; Mary, the elder, with a sort of clinging depend-
ence on her younger sister, and Sarah—Sarah, loved
in the deep, strong way of the saints. They met once
again, after Sister Mary Amadeus had been elected Superior of Toledo, and Mary would come to her like a little
child, laying her wants before her: "You are Superior,
Sarah. You can get me a copy of St. Jure and a black
apron, but as I'm allowed only one book, have all the
volumes bound in one, won't you, Sarah?" And Sarah
did.

Again, after her profession, our heroine goes up into
the mountain alone. She was always very silent about
the great graces of her life. This first year after her
profession, she seems to have spent in silent communion
with "The Beloved" in that continual interior mortification that forbids, but not in a forbidding way, communication of the most sacred joys. Father Faber says
every soul must have a secret she tells to no one. This
secret was the year that followed the profession of Sister
Mary Amadeus. There are whispers of some very
special communication with Our Lord, but these, even
the solemn stillness, the sacred majesty of the grave,
have not divulged. Still continuing the office of Syn-

dica, Sister Mary Amadeus spent her days in the school-
room both as mistress and teacher, weaving her wonderful influence about the children and winning their love
in an unequaled degree. How she could accomplish so
much, we can explain only by the sacrifice of much
sleep, and by the fact that she did everything so
well that she was never obliged to undo. For much
precious time is spent in undoing what we have blunder-
ingly done, in unraveling the tangled skein of mistakes.

Sometimes the older nuns worried about the future
of the young house. "Don't worry," Mother Alphonsus
would say. "All I have to do is to stand Sister Amadeus
on the street corner, and she will draw all the children
of Todelo."

In the meantime, Mary Warner, the schoolgirl friend
of Sister Mary Amadeus, had entered the Novitiate, giving the struggling community the help of her splendid
musical ability. Soon she donned the habit and the
name borrowed from Cleveland's sacred records, Annunciation. Mother Blessed Sacrament was filling the
house with the rich accents of her beautiful voice.
These three, Sisters Amadeus, Blessed Sacrament, and
Annunciation soon lifted Toledo out of its financial
stress.

On October 30, 1872, Edmund Dunne was married at
St. Philip du Roule, in Paris, to Josephine Beauharnais
Warner, sister to Mother Annunciation, and on April
16th, John Dunne was married at the Church of La
Madeleine, in Paris, to Miss Kate Stratton, only surviving daughter of Nelson Pitkin Stratton and Sarah Jane
Shepherd of Tulse Hill Brighton, London, England,
earlier of Waltham, Mass. Edmund, a brilliant orator,
became the leader of the Catholics in the vexed school

question, and John amassed a large fortune, and long ruled in the Philadelphia money market. Bright and beautiful children were born to both, and both were a source of the purest joy to their tender, loving sister. Another distinguished relative and friend also came to her, a man noted both as a student in Rome and as theologian and spiritual director in the Cleveland Diocese. Dr. Quigley, Pastor of St. Francis de Sales Church in Toledo, needs no tribute here. He was cousin to Mother Amadeus through the O'Dunnes of Palace and the O'Moores of Leix.

Dr. Quigley loved and revered his cousin, the brilliant young Ursuline, and unbent before her the rigid dignity of the "Standard Bearer of Right Versus Wrong." He was like a child before Sister Mary Amadeus, relying on her unerring judgment, chastened by the penance, the assiduity of the classroom.

Shadows fall athwart the sunniest path.

Mother Alphonsus had been everything to the Toledo Convent, and it had prospered under her strong rule. In 1869, she had obtained the ministry of the Rev. Jesuit Fathers as confessors and chaplains for her community. Chief among these were the Rev. Fathers Leiter and Eberschweiler. The former, "Anselmo" to Sister Mary Amadeus in the spiritual life; the latter, the guide of her footsteps in the steep ascent of superiority. Both preceded her to the grave, wonderful soul-secrets locked in their consecrated hearts. In 1870 she had built and opened the beautiful auditorium, and in 1873 the house was chartered.

But time was bringing too unmistakable signs of a painful cancer, and during the watches of her nights of suffering, the provident Superior would call her faithful, unsuspecting child to her bedside and begin to mold the young shoulders for the heavy burden she knew would soon fall upon them. Without letting her know it, Mother Alphonsus was preparing Sister Mary Amadeus to be the third Superior of Toledo Ursuline Convent.

The valiant, unselfish Superior, forgetful of her own intense pain, spoke, and the devoted young Sister listened, and tried to soothe her Superior's pain. The chapel, so beautiful in its chaste, artistic outline, had been begun, and all hoped against hope, that Mother Alphonsus would live to see it consecrated.

But Moses stood on the mountain top, and Aaron upheld his arms.

On July 19, 1874, the eighth Sunday after Pentecost, Mother Alphonsus, standing at her post in the Superior's stall, heard the words of the Gospel: "Thou canst be steward no longer." Suddenly, she was stricken with apoplexy. Hastily they carried her out, and laid her on the lounge in the parlor, and soon, without a word, the great woman was no more. Not a word to Sister Mary Amadeus, only that last look, that last sacred look that the future explains, so full is it of unspoken wisdom and tenderness.

Mother Immaculate Heart assumed the government of the house, and Sister Mary Amadeus was appointed to write a dispatch, announcing the death to the Bishop. Alas, her arm was temporarily paralyzed, and that night when, at last, the young hope of that stricken house removed her veil to go to bed, the beautiful brown hair was white as the driven snow.

Few words, intense feeling, that was Sister Mary Amadeus.

CHAPTER V

THE MAGNETIC YOUNG SUPERIOR

MOTHER ALPHONSUS was dead. The young community was in consternation. According to Rule, the first professed of the little band, Mother Immaculate Heart, as "Doyenne," took the reins of government until a canonical election could be held. What were they to do? Mother Alphonsus had been everything to them. Two nuns, Mother Immaculate Heart and Mother Xavier, who were in the infirmary, lay awake one night talking about their grief. One said: "What shall we do without Mother?" Then in the dread silence of the night, came the unexpected answer: "Keep silence," in the well-known voice of the great disciplinarian. They recognized them, these accents, commanding, and dear. Sister Mary Amadeus stood apart from all their plans and anxieties communing with her grief, entering deeper into the Heart of Him Who does not die, Who cannot abandon. She used to walk in the unfinished chapel and wish that "Mother" would come to her, too. But Mother did not come. The mysterious curtain flapped not outward. For the first time, she was appointed to teach a parochial school, and she used to walk silently, with her little lunch basket under her arms, across the river to St. Joseph's. Quite alone she kept, forgotten as she thought, and yet the nuns were talking about her, planning for her. She was so gentle, so strong, so magnetic and withal spiritual, with that true self-forgetting Ursuline spirituality. At meditation in the mornings,

41

Mother Alphonsus' cat used to steal into the chapel and sit at her feet. They say that a cat knows instinctively the head of the house, but Sister Mary Amadeus would drive it away with a caress, for she loved animals, too.

God had hidden her away, because He was preparing to lay upon her great honors and great burdens. He was fashioning her in silence and in sorrow. And the unconscious teacher of St. Joseph's school was attracting the hearts and the notice of the other religious, and the light of the Holy Ghost was playing about her, as she came and went, so sorrowful and yet so unselfish, as Mother Alphonsus' fit and most worthy successor.

At length dawned October 5, 1874, and Bishop Gilmour came to Toledo to hold the canonical election—the second great Bishop friend standing beside Sister Mary Amadeus. A short and simple ceremony it proved to be. In five minutes, the ballot came out, bearing the name "Sister Mary Amadeus" on every ticket except her own. She was unanimously chosen, this young and beautiful Ursuline, to succeed the great Mother Alphonsus. Yet she was not afraid. Buoyant she was, full of trust in God, fearless as St. Catherine of Sienna. God would help, that she knew. The nuns would stand by her from the first to the last. Bishop Gilmour and the Rev. Jesuit Fathers would guide and counsel her.

Of what should she be afraid? "Fear is afraid of Cæsar." In their grief, the Community of Toledo had promised that the successor of Mother Alphonsus should have the title "of the Heart of Jesus" added to her name, and this beautiful title was solemnly and lovingly conferred upon her whom we shall hereafter know as "Mother Amadeus of the Heart of Jesus."

The Community of Toledo was a blessed one. It was

one solidly compacted family, one in thought, in feeling, in ambition, in hope, each one sincerely loving, praising, upholding the other, whether she could bake a pie or teach a class in geometry. The great cloud was lifted; the sun was shining that October day, and they stepped bravely forth into the second phase of their existence, like a brother, leaning upon the arm of his brother. Why should they not succeed? And they did succeed. That night, when it became her duty to intone the blessing of the dormitory, Mother Amadeus began in her clear, courage-inspiring tone, when her schoolgirl friend, Mother Annunciation, facetiously slipped a book into her hand, reminding her that she had not yet attained the age when an Ursuline may officiate without the use of her office book.

Bishop Rappe, the first friend of the new Superior, consecrated October 7, 1847, had resigned in 1870, and retired to Burlington, Vermont, but he continued until the end to follow with his interest and his prayers the dear child of his heart. He rejoiced with an "I told you so" look in his eye when he heard of his namesake's election. Almost until the day of his death, he continued his missionary labors. His affability of manner, his winning character had made it possible for him to do great good in the diocese he had founded. He assembled five diocesan synods, founded three Ursuline Convents; at Cleveland, Toledo, and Tiffin, brought to his diocese the Jesuits and the Franciscans, and made the support of the parochial schools obligatory. Bishop Gilmour, the second friend of our heroine, was consecrated April 14, 1872. He was a man of strong, aggressive personality, a stanch friend, a brilliant speaker. He founded the *Catholic Universe,* freed Catholic school property from taxation, and, like his predecessor, made the obligation of supporting the Catholic schools so stringent that at the time of his death, April 13, 1891, Cleveland boasted more parochial schools than any other diocese of its size in the United States. He founded the Ursuline Convents of Youngstown, 1874; of Nottingham, 1877; and, through Bishop Brondel and the Toledo Convent, the Ursulines of Montana in 1884.

These were the men who befriended Mother Amadeus of the Heart of Jesus.

All went merry as a marriage bell in the Ursuline Convent of Toledo. The classrooms filled up, the house had to be enlarged. Wherever Mother Amadeus of the Heart of Jesus passed there was a smile of encouragement that reminded one of heaven.

Another friend now appears. Sister Catherine, one of the old nuns, who had charge of the Superior's room. This simple little cell at the head of the stairs was known as "The Sacred Heart Room," and hither did Sister Catherine convey her charge, the Rev. Mother Amadeus of the Heart of Jesus, on the night of October 5, 1874. "You are going to be my child," she said, in that tender German accent, "and I am going to take care of you." And how she did it! How many roses of her simple charity she strewed upon the ascending path. How she would cheer with her simple stories of the old country, whilst she ministered like a guardian angel. One morning, after a night of great pain, Mother was unable to rise, and Sister brought what she thought was a dose of salts, which proved, however, to be corrosive sublimate.

No sooner had Mother swallowed the dose than she knew what had happened. "Sister Catherine," she said, "this is poison. Call the priest and the doctor." Swiftly Sister Catherine flew at this behest, and with her went sorrow and consternation through the ranks of Toledo Convent. Some hastened to the Sacred Heart Room, and others to the chapel, and these were the wisest. The first thought of an Ursuline in sorrow and in joy is the chapel. Dr. Fisher came and administered an antidote. Father Eberschweiler came, but he found there was no need, thank God, for Extreme Unction.

Mother was out of danger, but the strong antidote had burned the lining of her stomach, and until a few months before her holy death, she suffered from continual and painful vomiting. Scarcely a night after that was sleep vouchsafed to the Spouse of the Crucified. Easy to write; but most hard to live!

The feast of the Immaculate Conception was approaching, her first as Superior. And on that day we record the first official act of her administration, the dedication of the convent chapel. She had finished it according to Mother Alphonsus' plans, and had paid for it. She was most eager to see it dedicated on this the feast she ever loved best.

What an eventful day was the Immaculate Conception!

That day, the convent had virtually been founded, and, in commemoration, every recreation since that day opened with the greeting: "Let us rejoice in this day which the Lord has made." On that day Mother Amadeus began her religious life; on that day also, her administration as Superior by the consecration of the chapel under the invocation of "The Sacred Heart." As far as any mere human can, she resembled and loved the Stainless One. So many used to say, upon seeing her for the first time: "That young Mother makes me think of the Blessed Virgin."

In 1875 Father Eberschweiler was appointed chaplain. To his ordinary duties he added that of instructing the novices in the Catechism of the Vows, and in the art of singing, in faultless and lofty style, the Plain Chant of the Church. This was twenty-eight years before the great "Motu Proprio." He and the young Superior were pioneers always. Marked by the characteristic thoroughness of his race, Father Eberschweiler, poet and musician, did well all that he did. He lent a strong arm to the young Mother. It was soul-stirring to see him at the organ, his fingers gliding over the keys, finding new treasures there; soul-stirring, too, it was to listen to his strong and solid spiritual direction, to see him live what he taught. He longed for the Indian missions. His name will occur in this story. There is a beautiful affinity in the souls Our Lord brings together in His service.

In 1876, Mother Amadeus built a new Novitiate and had it canonically erected. The ceremony of the opening took place on November 1st, Toledo being then the only convent in the United States where the Novitiate was organized and conducted according to the strict Normæ of the Church and of the Order. The novices were separated from the rest of the community and devoted exclusively to the study of the Office, the Rule, the exercises of the interior life, and their own spiritual formation, and Toledo soon reaped the blessed fruits of this most wise course in the lovely, sincere and simple perfection of its young members.

Two of these especially figure in the mission history: Mother Mary of the Angels, Mother Amadeus' pupil and novice, and Mother Francis, the first to whom she gave the cap. When this latter, as Christine Seibert, came over from Adrian, Michigan, to consult Mother about her vocation to a life her two sisters had embraced before her, she said: "I looked upon Mother's decision as God's, and I came without fear."

On September 8th died the saintly Amadeus Rappe, founder of the Ursuline houses of Ohio, and first Bishop of Cleveland. Great sorrow had made his death welcome to him and tolerable to his devoted friends and the children who revered him.

And in that same year, we find the energetic young Superior of Toledo honoring the Immaculate Conception once more on her beautiful feast day.

Favored from her youth with the gift of prayer which had been nurtured by her connection with the Ursulines of Boulogne, Mother Amadeus lived her schoolgirl and her religious life in close union with God. Strenuous activity at the call of obedience had not destroyed, in the depths of her heart, the spirit of cloister which is a characteristic mark of the Ursulines of the old school—an unmistakable mark which St. Angela had, from her little cell, at St. Affra's, burned into the hearts of those who were the very first to erect the cloister in their hearts, and to go among their fellowmen, as religious had never done before.

Mother Amadeus had long cherished in that heart where so many things beautiful and unsuspected lay hidden, a burning desire to restore the enclosure prescribed in 1607 for the Ursulines of Paris, if she could do so without hindering the work of the parochial schools. She had consulted Bishop Gilmour and had received his blessing and approval. For he was a pastor

of most large and noble mind, and she knew well how
to lay before him her plans, her hopes, her projects.
In order to carry out this great project she first
visited the old Monastery of Quebec. On this eventful
journey she was accompanied by her cousin, the
Rev. Dr. Quigley, and by Mother St. Agnes, one of the
counselors of the Toledo Convent.

Founded in 1635 by the Venerable Mary of the Incarnation, the Theresa of the New World, one hundred years
after St. Angela had given definite form to the Order at
Brescia, the Ursuline Convent of Quebec was in its two
hundred and fortieth year. The travelers were received
with enthusiasm, for the object of their visit made the
old heart of the monastery beat high with renewed and
quickened hope. They wondered at this young Superior of a prosperous house in what they called "Young
America," coming to drink at a fountain-head of mon-
asticism. The spring is ever bubbling up afresh; the
world has not yet found a better thing.

And the old Mothers were captivated by the entrancing amiability, the gentle magnetism of the Superioress of Toledo. They took her to their hearts,
showed her the old monastery, every corner of it, with
all its secrets, its archives, its relics, the chest with the
guimps worn by the foundress, Venerable Mary of the
Incarnation, so absolutely like her own. They gave her
practical hints about enclosure, its effects on the interior spirit. Truly is it a vision, the fresh young soul
that craves asceticism. Indeed the American character
is most fit for it, most ready with its straight, strong
principles, the intense respect for law, order and tradition. Witness the recent expansion of Carmel in our
land.

The impression Mother Amadeus made in Quebec remained. She prayed long at the tomb of Mary of the Incarnation. They wondered. Did they see the spirit of the older missionary descending upon the younger, awakening there the dreams of her school days? Did they hear "Montana," "Alaska" singing in her heart? Could they descry Jesus amid the glaciers, beckoning, beckoning?

God prepares His workers. He knows His own secrets.

When Mother Amadeus had sufficiently studied the matter in hand, she made a pilgrimage to St. Anne de Beaupré, and then sailed away amid the Thousand Islands back to Toledo. The great project was ripe in her heart and in her hands. She gave to it characteristic energy and tact, sparing neither time, trouble, nor expense. It was done, and done with the utmost perfection and in strict conformity to Rule. And the older nuns afterward said that, whilst they enjoyed the privilege of enclosure, they noticed in themselves an increase of the interior spirit, a joyous, buoyant interior life and deeper recollection, which are, I believe, the advantages of enclosure in our day, when the physical protection of the grates is no longer necessary. Convinced that this is the one thing necessary, Mother Amadeus would not have hesitated to give up all that she loved, even the Indian missions, for the sake of establishing the enclosure.

Thus, on December 8, 1878, was it restored in Toledo Convent. God blessed this act of generosity, for the very next year, 1879, a fresh productive field of labor was thrown open to the Ursulines.

The house of Youngstown, Ohio, founded by Cleveland, had struggled on through the first five years of its

existence. As the Mother House was not just then able
to supply the subjects needed, it was agreed that Toledo
should lend a helping hand. So Mother Amadeus, the
dauntless, the generous immolator of self—for she always gave and she always experienced the truth of the
"Date et dabitur"—sent seven of her own nuns,
who soon succeeded in putting the house on a good footing. The subsequent brilliant success of the Ursuline
Convent at Youngstown is due, under God, to her
great wisdom in the choice of the Superior Mother St.
Lawrence. Many such acts mark the life of Mother
Amadeus of the Heart of Jesus. She loved Mother St.
Lawrence, and counted upon her. In the secret soul to
soul intimacy that may be between Sister and Superior,
she had discovered unsuspected ability dormant in the
humble Mother St. Lawrence. The choice was a great
surprise to the community, but years of unselfish use-
fulness, the love of her Sisters, the unwonted and bril-
lant success of Youngstown Convent, justified Mother
Amadeus' choice.

Another great opportunity for good, for unselfish
helpfulness, offered itself in 1878. Under the leadership
of Mother Clara, seven Ursulines from Duren, in Germany, fleeing before the *"Kulturkampf,"* knocked at
Mother Amadeus' door and she received them. They
announced neither the day nor the hour of their coming,
and ignorant of American customs, they stood one day
helpless on the street corner. The cabdriver wanted to
charge one dollar apiece, and they were seven with many
parcels. The Superior alone spoke, and she only a very
few words in broken English. After an hour's wait in
doubt and anxiety, kind Providence came to their assistance in the person of an Ursuline pupil who spoke

Rev. E. W. J. Lindesmith, U. S. A.

German. She understood their sad plight, and hastened
to send word to Mother Amadeus that seven Ursulines
were standing out on the street corner. Soon was their
suffering exchanged for the most delicate and sisterly
welcome.

All that the exiles needed was supplied with lavish
love. The two communities lived like one, the two Superiors like Sisters. Who but Mother Amadeus would act
thus? Her heart was fearless and trustful, and the
Divine Banker, she knew, would not fail her. After
the German Ursulines had founded their own prosperous house, the nuns kept up the friendliest relations in
that deep gratitude that knows not time, and in their
letters they would tell and tell again the impression
made on them by the generosity, the magnetism of
"Dear Mother Amadeus of the Heart of Jesus." Few
Superiors indeed would have offered hospitality such as
hers. The German community was at home, protected,
at leisure to arrange for the future prosperity which
did indeed come. When they left, Mother Amadeus sent
with them one of her best young teachers that she might
help them until they had learned English. What exquisite delicacy and generosity was this. Here, too, we
must chronicle a passing visit from the great Mother
Hardy, with her companion, Mother Hoey, of the Ladies
of the Sacred Heart who, after a few days beneath
Mother's roof, added their word of praise for her hospitality.

In 1879, the nuns joyously celebrated the twenty-
fifth anniversary of the foundation of their dear house.
Mother obtained a solemn triduum, and Exposition of
the Most Blessed Sacrament, and spent many hours upon
her knees, motionless, wrapt in the joy of thanksgiving.

4448

It was a wonderful sight to see Mother Amadeus of the
Heart of Jesus before the Most Blessed Sacrament exposed. A wonderful protection wrapped the house
around whilst the Superior prayed and garnered light
and strength for herself and for all. Nuns and children
cast furtive glances at her in those sacred hours, glances
full of awe and reverence. No one has ever read their
secrets, but secrets there were. One thought came often
from Mother Amadeus' heart to her grateful lips. The
classrooms, the Novitiate had filled to overflowing,
though she had never refused a request made to her,
and yet during all these years there had been but one
death, that of the foundress. Rugged, cheerful poverty,
enclosure and austerity had blossomed health and prosperity to the "Home, Sweet Home." She ruled like
a queen, the queen of hearts and minds whose word was
always unquestioned because full of wisdom. No tyr-
anny, no fear, no compulsion, only wisdom and trust
on the part of the magnetic young Superior, and love and
generous co-operation on the part of the nuns.

Verily it seemed that never a shadow could fall on
Toledo Convent and on Mother Amadeus of the Heart of
Jesus. But never a saint was made in the sunshine.

CHAPTER VI

A Change

MOTHER ALPHONSUS had held sway beyond the years appointed by Rule. Why should not Mother Amadeus? Her rule had been one of love and triumphant success. The house was still comparatively young. Why should not Mother Amadeus continue in charge? She had been unanimously elected in 1874, and unanimously re-elected in 1877. Why not again in 1880? That is what the vocal religious thought, the vocal religious, all but one. The great Mother Amadeus, large, far-seeing, and utterly oblivious of self, knew that Toledo had a rich, rare gem locked in its heart—a talisman: the love of Rule. And to the Rule must be sacrificed all personal feelings. She, therefore, with her irresistible will, silenced all these plausible. arguments, and set about preparing for the triennial election.

Among her spiritual children, was one whom she deemed fit for the charge, Mother Stanislaus Duffy, and her she recommended to all who sought her advice, or spoke to her, trembling and fearful, about the election.

Why should they fear, sweet Mother Amadeus said. When Mother Alphonsus died, they were satisfied with her, and now that she had been six years in charge, there was Mother Stanislaus, and they had God and the Rule.

Mother did not know it, but as Our Lord had hidden her amid her Sisters at the death of Mother Alphonsus to prepare her for the coming labors, so He hid her

53

again now to prepare her for the mission life: "a cloud received her out of their sight."

Mother Stanislaus was elected, and Mother Amadeus of the Heart of Jesus, the great Mother Amadeus of the Heart of Jesus, became, at first, Mistress of Novices, and then Syndica. Quietly, silently, she performed her allotted task. God was fashioning His great missionary, preparing to draw from the sacred soil of that virgin heart that exquisite flower that had shown its tiny cotyledons in the recreation grounds of Cleveland, when Sarah Theresa Dunne would suddenly stop in the race, and say to her wondering playmates: "I shall be a missionary in the Rocky Mountains and in Alaska some day. Yes? You will all see."

Why are we so petulant? So anxious? "Beyond the dim unknown, standeth God within the shadow, keeping watch above His own." He will do it. Yes. But slowly and wisely and well. There are some scenes in every life, but especially in the lives of the Saints, which can be read only by the light of faith. Why, and how, some things happen is beyond our natural power to see and understand. But when we look back upon the best actions of our lives, and find them marked by the cross, we begin to understand that they are God-sealed, that His ways are not ours, and that He wants the sweetest fruits all for Himself.

During Mother Amadeus' time in the Novitiate as Mistress, occurred, in 1883, the death of Sister St. Bernard, a pupil of the Sacred Heart, Manhattanville, a rare soul, who leaned on Mother's sturdier spiritual growth. In dying, she promised to obtain from Our Lord financial help for all Mother's future labors. Nor, though she suffered great poverty and anxiety, was

Mother Amadeus ever without the necessary means to carry on her wonderful labors for the salvation of souls.

Bishop Gilmour, the straight, strong man, the changeless friend, admired and supported Mother Amadeus. He and she were built on a like, large mold, and he watched, in silence, her conduct during her years of retirement, and remembered it.

Whither will the mysterious finger of God point next?

The Cheyenne Indians of Eastern Montana are known among the Tribes as "The Aristocrats." They are the last of the great Algonquin family to be Christianized. At this time, they were giving the United States Government great trouble. From time immemorial, they had lived on the fertile banks of the winding Tongue River. Its verdant acclivities were unspeakably dear to these proud "Auctothones," unspeakably sacred, for upon them blanched the bones of their ancestors. Just when the Cheyennes settled on Tongue River, it is impossible to tell. They themselves say: "Oh, it was long ago." The year 1876 is the high-water mark of their history, for in that, to them, melancholy year, on June 25th, they took their stand, four thousand two hundred strong, beside the Sioux in the bloody fight by the "Little Big Horn," and it was the Cheyenne "Rain in the Face" who uttered and executed the fearful threat, prompted by great admiration, that he would eat Tom Custer's heart, which he did in less time than it takes to write it, the Indians cutting down every man of the two hundred and sixty brave followers of General Custer.

The Cheyennes stood in line against Creek, McKenzie, and Miles, and when, in 1879, the Government attempted to move them down into the Indian Territory, "White Bull," "Red Cloud," and seven other chiefs stoutly refused to go. Some Cheyennes are still to be found in Indian Territory, but the main body of the migrators, dissatisfied and rebellious, fought their way back, inch by inch, to the land of their birth under the shadows of the hills where sleep their forefathers. This raid, which was remarkable for its brutality, is known as "the bloody trail," and reminds us of the "Flight of the Tartar Tribes" in the eighteenth century. Though far less in numbers, still they had to battle with the obstacles of a more advanced civilization, a denser population, more enlightened opponents. The Cheyennes murdered and pillaged all along their way until the name "Black Wolf" and "Fire Crow" made the settlers tremble. Swooping down upon lonely villages at night, they murdered young and old without mercy, taking the women prisoners—one of these was still to be seen in Black Wolf's camp in 1884—pinning their victims to the ground with sharp pointed stakes and throwing corpses over the fences, bloody landmarks of their passage.

This was in 1879, the day of speeding railroads and buzzing telegraph wires. And still the Cheyennes marched on, passng through three States, crossing four railroads, with telegraph lines in full operation, and leaving behind them a trail of fire and of blood, the like of which is unknown in history, until at length, in 1882, they were stopped by General Miles, and allowed to return to the site of their own choosing, ceded to them by the Government since 1902.

Still these fierce Cheyennes were amenable to kindness, and God was preparing for them the fruits of His redemption, through the gentle, tactful, wise, straightforward Mother Amadeus of the Heart of Jesus.

The kindness of General Miles to these Indians, his honest dealing, too, his wisdom in securing the friendship of Okowokomas (White Bull), their chief, did more than powder and ball to quiet these wild children of the plains. But they were still restless, and the authorities were ill at ease.

At the nearest military post, Fort Keogh, near Miles City, Montana, was a man according to God's own heart. a man who had made his mark in the West, the Rev. Elias Washington John Lindesmith. When questioned about his initials, E. W. J., he used to answer that he bore the name of the greatest patriarch of the Old Testament, the greatest prophet of the New, and of the Father of his country. He was a soldier, every inch of him, who could boast forty-seven blood relations in his country's ranks from the Revolution down through the War of 1812, the Seminole, Civil and Spanish Wars. Zealous beyond all possibility of praise, he spent all the time left him from his military duties as chaplain of Fort Keogh, scouring Southeastern Montana, where he was the only Catholic priest, dressed in his buckskin suit, mounted upon his indefatigable steed, searching for recruits for the army of the Lord. He held within his hands the hearts of all who knew him, so upright was he. His heart was innocent and pious as that of a child, withal he was strong, a very knight of the Lord, fighting His battles on the outskirts of civilization. Father Lindesmith was a friend to cherish, an opponent to dread, and the respect he commanded everywhere was equaled only by the love he won.

"I was thinking, Your Reverence," said to him one

Yoakam, a fervent, practical Catholic, as he doffed his hat when the man of God one day rode past the field he was plowing. "I was thinking, if you could only get some Sisters among these wild ones, the Cheyennes, they could do more for the Government than a regiment," and as Father Lindesmith rode on, the thought thus expressed to him took root in his heart and budded speedily into action. He determined at once to submit the project to proper authority.

Another great actor in this epic for the conquest of souls now appears: John Baptist Brondel, the third great Bishop of our biography. God raised up John Baptist Brondel, the missionary Bishop by excellence, to make possible the Indian Missions of Montana.

John Baptist Brondel was born in the old lace-making, bell-ringing town of Bruges on February 23, 1842, in one of those patriarchial families where saints are bred. His vocation to the Indian missions was as marked as his vocation to the holy priesthood. For the finger of another great man was beckoning to him from afar, and speaking to him in the deep silence of his heart. There is no drama like the one God has written: the vocation of chosen souls. How the actors come in, one by one, from the uttermost ends of the earth at His bidding!

Father de Smet, the great Indian missionary, was at this time evangelizing with unequaled success, the Indian tribes beyond the Mississippi, and all Catholic Europe was resounding with his praises. One night, when Mrs. Brondel sat knitting by the lamp, the cloth having been removed from the supper table, the father of the family looked over his spectacles and said to his eldest son: "Charles, read to us from the *Annals of the*

Propagation of the Faith the letters of the great missionary in America." And as the older boy read aloud, little John Baptist sat hidden in the huge fireplace beside the crackling log, where he could see the stars even in the daytime. "Oh!" said this brave little heart to itself, "some day, I, too, shall be a missionary, and I shall go to those Indians. But I must not tell anyone. They would feel too bad."

And the lad grew up and was proficient in his studies. A lovable nature was his, whose deep thoughts spoke in the eloquence of a most musical voice. When he was sixteen, he knocked at the door of the Capuchin Convent of his native city. He was told that he was too young to don the cowl, and that, besides, no religious might demand to be sent to one field rather than to another.

So the undaunted missionary determined to be true to his Indian vocation, and he turned instead to the American College of Louvain. Nor was his vocation weakened by his association with the saintly Charles Seghers, the martyr and apostle of Alaska, whom he was to succeed in the mission and in the episcopal see of Victoria. To no one else had young John Baptist mentioned his missionary vocation. Late one afternoon, however, shortly before ordination, he and two of his fellow-students went out for a last long walk together. Their conversation naturally drifted toward the future —one would be a Dominican, the other a Jesuit. John Baptist was silent. "And you, John Baptist," they queried, "we can get no clue to your mysterious vocation." At length, the fervent young deacon broke the long silence. "I am going to follow Father Seghers into the Mission of Western North America."

And, in after years, when he went back as Bishop
to his native land, he met these friends. Each had been
faithful to the lofty pre-ordination purpose.

On All-Hallows eve, 1866, Father Brondel reached
his first destination, Vancouver, B. C. He labored successfully there and at Steilacoom on Puget Sound, Walla
Walla, Olympia, and Tacoma until 1879, when, on December 14th, he was consecrated Bishop of Victoria by
his friend and predecessor in that see, Archbishop
Seghers. On March 7, 1884, he was transferred to the
Vicariate Apostolic of Montana, of which, on July 2,
1884, he became first Bishop. Great Archbishop Seghers
of Portland asked, and obtained, permission to go back
to Victoria that he might labor once more among his
dear Eskimos of Alaska. When Bishop Brondel told
this dear friend of his appointment, the martyr ad-
vised him in the words of the day's gospel, telling him to
imitate her who *"abiit in Montana cum festinatione."*

On that day, thirty-eight years before, was born the
woman destined by God to help the new Bishop in his
labors in the cause of Catholic education, the sweet
subject of our biography, and the lines of these two
lives began to run parallel, nor were they ever to
diverge.

It was to Bishop Brondel that Father Lindesmith
communicated the words of Yoakum, the pioneer, and
the Bishop at once set about bringing the words to
fruition.

Bishop Brondel wrote at once to his brother Bishops
east of the Mississippi, begging for help in the organization of the new diocese, and one of them understood,
and came to his assistance.

CHAPTER VII

A Journey Big With Possibilities

Six Start for Montana

BISHOP GILMOUR, on October 20, 1883, wrote, through the columns of the *Catholic Universe*, an open letter to the Religious of his diocese, asking for volunteers to go to evangelize the Cheyenne Indians of Montana. This letter was eagerly read by the Ursulines of Toledo and, on October 21st, Feast of St. Ursula, thirty of these great-hearted Religious, among whom was Mother Amadeus, sent their names to Bishop Gilmour. God's elective affinities are indeed wonderful!

Their Bishop came to them that day, proud of his Ursulines. The Most Blessed Sacrament was exposed. It was the patronal feast, the high light of missionary fervor. Not unlike was this scene to the one enacted in the Ursuline Convent of Tours in 1639, when the Venerable Mother Mary of the Incarnation, and one companion hovered about the grate to obtain permission to follow Madame de la Peltrie to Canada. By a sort of spiritual atavism, traits repeat themselves in the story of the saints. Out of the thirty names, Bishop Gilmour selected six. To Mother Amadeus, he said: "I appoint you Superior General of all the houses you may found in Montana." "My Lord," she replied, "what are these houses to be?" "Whatever you make them." "And whence their support?" further queried Mother Amadeus. "My child, God never sent a bird out

61

into the forest without caring for it. How much more
will He care for you." And that was all. Thus was
the momentous question settled, between two great
souls strong of faith.

Bishop Gilmour, the man of action, wrote at once to
Bishop Brondel: "I am sending you six Ursulines for a
Christmas present, and Mother Amadeus, the flower of
my flock, is at their head." From that day on, the convent was a scene of busy preparation, and many were
the lamentations, the complaints from friends unnumbered. "What, Mother Amadeus to leave Toledo? No,
never. We shall not allow it." But Bishop Gilmour
was not a man to be trifled with, and God was whisper-
ing to Mother's heart as to St. Paul's on the road to
Damascus: "I will show thee how great things thou
must suffer for My name's sake." Time sped swiftly by
from St. Ursula's day to the day of departure. And it
was well that it did. January 15th dawned. The Sunday before, Bishop Gilmour, the generous, had had a col-
lection taken up in all the churches of the city to defray
the expenses of the journey to Montana. That morning
the community were up betimes. Meditation, Mass,
Holy Communion, breakfast, and the swift good-byes
in which stout hearts swallow tears with smiling coun-
tenances, and the six missionaries walked bravely from
the door to the coaches that were to convey them to the
railroad station. Rev. Eyler, the future Montana chaplain, Mother Stanislaus, and a crowd of friends followed
them until the station was a mass of moving flowers.
Was the first lady of the land boarding the west-bound
train? No, it was Mother Amadeus, the beloved of Catholic Toledo's heart.

Tearful eyes, too, were following from behind the

sacred enclosure into the unknown, whilst they themselves, these dear missionaries, looked on with absolute trust in Divine Providence.

The community grieved, yet felt honored, and kept repeating the words of the Ursulines of Tours in 1639: "Is it possible that God has destined our house for so great an honor?" As far as Mother Amadeus was concerned, no one was surprised. They had long felt a secret presentment that God would draw her out of the enclosure for the accomplishment of some great work.

CHAPTER VIII

MONTANA

On January 17th, in the year of Our Lord, 1884, a
train pulled into the cowboy city, named after General Miles. The thermometer registered 40° below zero.
Here were the Ursulines to establish their first headquarters, and here, standing upon the platform, to bid them
welcome, was their own dear Bishop with the Rev. E. W.
J. Lindesmith at his side. Bishop Brondel had come
the five hundred miles from Helena to greet the Ursulines, and there he stood exact to his word as he always
proved. How deeply touched were the Ursulines by this
first proof of paternal benevolence! And here begins
the long, sweet story.

Bishop Brondel was proud to show this, his priceless
Christmas gift from Bishop Gilmour to the Montanians.

The celebrated incorporated cowboy town, Miles City,
numbered, in 1884, 2,500 inhabitants. It boasted a few
pretty garden homes, two stores of general merchandise,
two business streets, and sixty-five saloons. It was the
centre of rolling farm and pasture lands, and there were
precious veins of black diamond in the buttes about.
The motley gathering, in which the cowboy predominated, in chaps and sombreros, booted and spurred,
hailed the nuns with delirious enthusiasm, and those
gathered about the saloons doffed their sombreros,
removed their pipes, and observed a reverential silence
when the nuns, with lowered veils, walked past.

But whether this outward demonstration had taken

the place of a more practical kindness, or whether one relied on the other, and no one knew how to go about it, the fact is that no provision had been made to receive the nuns, and the Ursulines found themselves on that cold January 17th homeless and alone.

Strange as the fact may seem in itself, it ceases to be so when we look at the supernatural side of the story, so oft repeated in God's greatest works. He was to do it all Himself, and He began by giving it His blessing, the blessing of the cross. So, after a few moments consultation with the Bishop and Father Lindesmith, no one having offered them a night's lodging, Mother Amadeus led her nuns to the boarding house of one widow McCanna. Her home, she boasted, was made of logs, each one of which had been dragged from the mountains at the cost of five dollars, and, with much Gaelic exuberance, she conducted the six distinguished ladies from Toledo to the only vacant room in the house. Alas, this shelter was neither clean nor warm. The nuns could not occupy the bed, so they sat down on the floor in a semi-circle, their backs against the wall, as Barbara Fontana and St. Angela used to do. Of course, they could not sleep; they had had no supper, for their hostess had brought them a few herring bones swimming in dubious water, and besides, the partition against which leaned their tired heads, was the partition also of a laundry run by one Gee Lee, a Chinaman, whom some of the nuns, in their first burst of missionary zeal, mistook for an Indian. Moreover, the cowboys domiciled in the rest of the little house, thinking, of course, as men do, that the "Lady Black Robes" were comfortably lodged for the night, gave way to traditional conviviality and hilarity. Sounds strange and various reach the ear of God, but there is not the slightest little breath of prayer that He rejects. And this first night of suffering He accepted for the welfare of the Ursuline missions.

The next morning, as soon as the first streaks of dawn purpled the streets, the nuns left the house, and began to cut the first of their many trails through the deep snow to the church. The night had turned it into a very block of ice. They unlocked it, and with hands frozen and unused to such labor, they gathered chips and made a big blazing fire. When the Bishop appeared in the sanctuary at 8 A. M., he was greeted by a genial warmth, the symbol of all his future dealings with Mother Amadeus and the Ursulines. His heart was glad, and when he turned after the Gospel to speak, it was with the sweet musical eloquence of heart and voice. Yes, his voice was mellow, his accents fervid, and he reminded the nuns that on that very day, years ago, St. Peter had come to Rome, unknown and a stranger, as they, too, had come into the wilderness of Montana. Whilst he spoke, he and they were choked with emotion at seeing the wonderful ways of God. Oh! what a Communion was that. Our Lord is always entrancing, but to the heart of the missionary! *"Expertus potest dicere."*

After their long thanksgiving, they walked back two by two to the house at five dollars a log. The Bishop and Mother took the lead, and began the first of their many subsequent conversations on business. Bishop Brondel listened like a wise, kind father whilst Mother Amadeus explained how impossible it was for them to remain in their present quarters. She, with one of the nuns, would go about looking for a modest home they

Rt. Rev. J. B. Brondel, First Bishop of Montana.

might call a convent. So, after swallowing a cup of
poor coffee, Mother, with characteristic energy and
promptness, set about accomplishing her undertaking.
The most difficult part of it all, was to break the news
to Mrs. McCanna's kind heart without wounding its
sensibilities. She had indeed done her best, and the
nuns were most grateful to her for the night's shelter.
Mother Amadeus' kind heart, her exquisite tact, made
it all right with the hostess when she explained the
exigencies of Rule, and their purpose of opening a
boarding school.

And with all the blessings of the Gael called down
upon her, Mother Amadeus and her companions started
out. Until late in the afternoon, they walked the
little town holding a map and guided by Mr. Court-
ney, the town site agent, who afterward proved so true
a friend. They found a little four room house on
Pleasant Street which Mother Amadeus fearlessly
lessly rented at thirty dollars a month. Her trust in
Providence was ever unbounded. Later a distinguished
Jesuit said, in speaking of her: "What I liked best
in Mother Amadeus was her fearlessness in undertaking
great things for God." Carrying in their hands little
parcels of coal, matches, coffee, potatoes, ten cents worth
of each, they returned for their anxious companions.
A stove had to be bought, and they were alone, stran-
gers, and no one came forward to help them.

Mother St. Francis installed herself as chief operator,
and when, finally, the stove was up, and the fire burning, they all went out into the snow, to see the
smoke go curling up to heaven from the first
Ursuline Convent in Montana. They had brought six
buffalo robes with them, and these they stretched upon

the floor about the stove, for beds, but before they lay
down upon these Capuan couches, they went about the
bare house singing the words of St. Francis: "This is
true joy! This is true joy!"

Sunday dawned, the feast of the Holy Name of Jesus.
It was January 20th, and these cloistered religious would
have to receive Holy Communion at High Mass before
the assembled Miles City congregation. They rose early,
some had used satchels, others Webster's dictionary,
whilst Rand's Atlas of the World had been picked out,
as the best pillow, for Mother's downy couch. Sacrifice
seemed so easy, so attractive, the buoyancy in the heart
of the foundress was catching. The divine had stolen
into the unconscious human instruments.

They were busy in church until Mass; then a long
sermon, Holy Communion, thanksgiving, then hurry
home to attend to the Bishop's breakfast. And at
length, at two that afternoon, kneeling about their
trunk—they had neither table nor chairs—they prepared to break their long fast with a cup of coffee, a
slice of dry bread. First they listened with tearful eyes
to the first letter from home. "Not by bread alone doth
man live." And Mother Stanislaus had written, enclosing
thirty dollars—the first month's rent. She told them to
expect a box of biscuits, but to be careful not to break
their teeth if they proved hard. And when the gift
came, behold another month's rent baked in the morsel.
And as God feeds the sparrows and clothes the lilies,
so did He ever, just at the hour of greatest anxiety,
lay before the wonderful Mother Amadeus of the Heart
of Jesus, just what she needed for the hour. The very
poor alone can tell what gratitude is: visions of Providence, the purpling light of the dawn of hope. "God,"

she often said with President Lincoln, "must love the
plain people—He made so many of them."

Now began for Mother Amadeus and her nuns the
poetry of privation. In spite of the generosity of the
dear and magnanimous Mother Stanislaus, who had
sent, amongst other things, five Knabe pianos, and rich
velvet hangings for their little chapel, lack of money
made them suffer keenly for the want of the simplest
necessities. Montana air is bracing, a tonic, an appe-
tizer. They were very hungry at meals, their beds were,
not to put too fine a point upon it, hard, and they were
undoubtedly very hungry when they sat down to the
scantily furnished table, their rations, short rations of
corn meal, and a half dozen oranges which a dealer
brought because "They were rotten. I cannot sell
them." And Mother Amadeus had gone to the parlor
to thank him in her gracious way. She, above all, knew
how to thank, and the giver went away thinking she had
indeed conferred a great favor on "that wonderful
Mother." And the nuns only laughed at the table, and
passed the bread plate about saying: "I'm not hungry."
It was only very much later, that the secret of their actual need became known. Father Lindesmith one day
met a little girl running breathless through the streets.
He stopped her and asked her errand. "I am going to the
butcher shop to buy ten cents worth of liver for the
nuns," she said, and hurried on. And the great heart
was touched and "ten cents worth of liver for the nuns"
became the text of the following Sunday's sermon, and
with it the bitter need came to an end. The simple
chronicle is rich in God's poetry.

Soon Bishop Brondel sent Mother the deed for a
piece of property in the Leighton addition to Miles City,

on the north side of the Yellowstone, a block 500 by 500 feet. The nuns began to unpack their great Toledo-packed trunk and to get ready for their first boarders. They decked their chapel, but so tiny was it that when saying the "Gloria" at Office, their heads often touched and they would be seized with laughter, these uncon-scious heroines. The Indians from Tongue River used to come down to see Mother, the "Makamahehonawihona" (the great holy, white chief woman), and she would lead them to the Blessed Sacrament, make them kneel down and repeat the Holy Name of Jesus, and her virgin heart would light up with the joy a mother knows at her child's first distinct utterance.

Before leaving the nuns, the Bishop had, on the feast of the martyr St. Agnes, placed the Most Blessed Sacra-ment in their tabernacle, and the first Ursuline Convent of Montana was founded. Nor was the "Holy Reserve" anywhere else in the town, for Father Lindesmith lived at Fort Keogh, and said Mass in the church only on Sundays.

The Cheyenne Indians loved Mother from the first. She had promised them that she would soon come to live with them on Tongue River, and they used to follow her reverently into the chapel, sit beside her when she said the Office, rising with the nuns and bowing their heads at the Gloria with all the graceful ceremonial of the race. And this was consolation for all the priva-tions until then endured.

Jealously did the Ursulines watch over the Lord's one trysting place in the Yellowstone valley. That spring, the river flooded its banks, and rose so high that the danger became most alarming. Father Lindesmith could not get away from the Post, so he sent Mother the following dispatch: "Fort Keogh, Montana. Mother Amadeus. Go to the church and take the Blessed Sacrament with you. E. W. J. Lindesmith, Chaplain, U. S. A."

Jealously did Mother watch the rising waters, not fearing, nay, rather almost hoping that they would invade her domain, and that she might fly into Egypt as Mary did, bearing her Lord in her arms, but the waters subsided, and the routine of convent life was not disturbed.

One night in Miles City, when the nuns had retired to rest, each on her buffalo robe, with book or satchel for downy pillow, violent knocking was heard at the door. Visions of frontier violence arose before their minds Mother Amadeus whose rug was always against the door for just such an emergency, rose promptly and called: "Who is there?" whilst the nuns quickly removed the poor beds. "A drummer for the Catholic Church," came back in response, in Father Guidi's well-known voice, and they threw open their little door, joyously to welcome the first Jesuit they had seen in Montana.

Sweet and simple are the joys, the annals of the missions.

The first pupils began to come, and with their parents, to pour out upon Mother the generous love that had greeted her everywhere. On February 2d, the Ursulines opened school with thirty-one boarders. Mother St. Francis taught the boys in the church, whilst Mother St. Ignatius, at the convent, astonished the girls by her wonderful erudition.

The very first of these most dear boarders were Lizzie, Nellie, and Jessie Wyman, daughters of Major

Wyman, United States agent at the Crow Reservation, and Lula, Lottie, and Minnie Price, daughters of the bandmaster at Fort Keogh. Never did children love their school as did these first precious ones in Montana.

In the early days, they miraculously escaped a fire which threatened the destruction of the tiny home. Mother Amadeus scented it, aroused the nuns and had it out ere children and neighbors were aware. Whilst Mother was up and about, fire, like all other evils, feared and fled her. Postulants came and nuns from Ohio, Missouri, New York, and so was the little Ursuline tree firmly rooted in Montana soil, and Mother Amadeus looked forward to keeping her promise to the Cheyennes on Tongue River.

CHAPTER IX

The Promise Kept

The Mission Tree Puts Forts Its Branches

On March 30, 1884, Feast of St. Amadeus, her first feast in the missions, Mother Amadeus started, with Bishop Brondel and three nuns destined to labor there, to open the mission in the Tongue River Reservation. Father Eyler had gone on ahead. They were tendered a Government ambulance, drawn by Government mules, and accompanied by an escort of six soldiers from Fort Keogh. So queenly was Mother Amadeus of the Heart of Jesus, that no favor could be refused her. She herself was so generous, and generosity, begetting generosity, marks the mission history from the very beginning. Missions multiplied and grew by division, as the waters grow more fruit—bearing as you spread them.

Evidently the joyous ebullition of these early days had not yet subsided. For, starting out on their first Indian mission, and ignorant of the nature of Montana travel, they had absolutely forgotten to provide a lunch for their honored guest and themselves. Their attention was rudely awakened to the fact, when a basket of fresh eggs was handed them at the first road ranch they passed. In vain did they scan the horizon and the treeless landscape, with here and there a hillock and soldiers' butte ahead, whilst Miles City vanished in the background. The sun had climbed up to the zenith, and a dreamy radiance lay upon the prairie. What were they to do?

A hotel forsooth in the plains of Montana?

Confusion worse confounded. But the Bishop, himself the pattern of missionaries, showed them what to do. Breaking an egg on the wheels of the ambulance, he swallowed it lustily, and made them do the same, whilst he laughed heartily at the dainty eastern ladies traveling in the mountains and expecting to meet at convenient distances, hotels and warm dinners. Raw eggs, this was the first meal in the Tongue River country— the first and the last time that they were taken unawares.

For two days, they followed the wide, open country with its misty lights and distant buttes, its exuberance of cactus growth, and now and then the outline of a mounted Cheyenne, practising wireless telegraphy, against the distant horizon. The first night they rested at Garland P. O. This typical road ranch, in a bend of the Tongue River and surrounded by cottonwood trees, was kept by one Mr. Ritz and his wife, and was enlivened by uncounted little tow-heads, who came in, wondering and silent at first, then captivated by the charm of this Mother, "The Mother." This was their first night in what might really be called "The Wilderness," with the distant call of the coyote, the hoot of the owl, and the incessant "lap, lap" of the caressing Tongue River. For the one-storied house was the only one of the station, and the solitude was intense. Especially did it seem so in the poetic utterances of the early morning, when the nuns rose and transformed their room into a chapel, and the Bishop found it ready for Mass when he knocked at the door. Were the Ursulines never to be found unprepared except in the matter of lunches for hungry travelers in the prairie?

At six o'clock in the morning of April 1st, they had had Mass, Holy Communion, and a good breakfast, a lunch packed by good Mrs. Ritz, and were off betimes for what is now St. Labre's Mission. Often were they obliged to dismount and walk while the soldiers pushed the ambulance up the acclivities, and nine times did they ford Tongue River. The "Witanoe"—the Cheyennes say—"because it is tortuous and crooked as a white man's tongue." At last, they reached its secluded stillness. A very necessary adjunct was the military escort Mother Amadeus had provided, for the devious road in and about hillocks was most inviting to "hold ups," by no means a thing of the past in 1884.

Eighty miles north of Miles City, in Southeastern Montana, separated from the Crow Reservation by the Wolf Mountains, bounded on the north by Stebbins Creek, on the south by Hanging Woman Creek, on the east by Tongue River, on the west by the Rosebud, the Cheyenne Reservation measures some twenty by twenty-five miles.

Here, in a bend of the river, stretches east and west beneath the watchful stars, the little line of low log cabins that was to become the first mission house of the Ursulines of Montana. They were three in number, these little cabins, not connected, flat mud roof, mud floor, one door, one window, the largest measuring sixteen by twenty-two feet. Palatial, the residence seemed to Mother and the nuns, and together they knelt down and kissed the threshold of "Lady Poverty," thanking God that they had been judged worthy to follow Christ, the Lord, in the utter nakedness and privation of true mission life.

"Ottowokomas" came forward to greet the Bishop, to bid his friend, "Makemahehonawihona" (the holy white chief woman), welcome.

"There is a mountain," said Old Wolf, the Cheyenne poet, to the Bishop. "There is a mountain in the neighborhood, known to every Cheyenne. It is high and strong, and many years old. Also our forefathers knew it. When children, we went out hunting, not caring whether we knew the way or not. When men, we went to meet the enemy, no matter whence he came. Though our way ran through heights and depths, our hearts trembled not on account of the road, because the mountain was ever a safe guide to us, and never missed its way. When far away, we saw the mountain, our hearts swelled with joy, because it was the messenger that told us our native place came nearer.

"True, often was the mountain attacked. In summer, the thunder shook it from top to foot, and fire bored holes in its sides, but the noise passed, and the mountain stood forever. In winter, the snowstorm rushed all around it, and covered its sides with thick layers. With difficulty could we distinguish it from other mountains. Only its height told us it was our mountain. But during spring all the snow disappeared, and the mountain stood covered with green grass before us as of yore, and the trees thereon stood firmer.

"*This mountain is the priest.* Whites and Indians speak ill of him. They wish to estrange him from our hearts, but we know that he has but one word, and that his heart is like a rock. He comes to instruct us, and what the mountain is in our journeys, that is his word. *He is the mountain that leads us to God.*"

No small honor to Bishop Brondel, that he inspired these words of the Cheyenne Goldsmith:

"But all his serious thoughts had rest in heaven
As some tall cliff that lifts its awful form,
Swells from the vale and midway leaves the storm,
Though around its breast the rolling clouds are spread,
Eternal sunshine settles on his head."

The poetic ceremonial over, the nuns began busily to prepare for the first night. The farthest cabin was the residence of the Father, and there the Bishop found shelter as best he could. The middle cabin was given to the Most Blessed Sacrament, curtained off during the day for the nuns' living room. The largest cabin was the school-room, benches moved in during the day and buffalo robes at night. And when Mother Amadeus and the nuns lay down they who had said on entering, "how low the ceiling is," went to sleep exclaiming, "how high the ceiling is," for they forgot they were lying on the bare ground. And every now and again they rose and peeped out of their little window to watch the Cheyennes on the hill across the river, dancing to the moon to thank her for bringing them the nuns.

The next day, April 2d, Feast of St. Richard, sacred because of Bishop Gilmour, they rose betimes, threw their beds across the fence—alas! a coyote one day devoured one of them—brought in the benches for school, made their meditation, and prepared the tiny chapel for Mass. For the Bishop, in the Government ambulance, was to make an early start back to Miles City; the escort was preparing the teams. They must hear the Bishop's Mass, receive the Bread of the Strong, hear the Mass of thanksgiving, make ready His Lordship's breakfast, and receive his blessing before he left them. And when he stood on the banks of the beautiful river, he spoke a few kind words to them. They had, he said, the children and the Most Blessed Sacrament, and that is all an Ursuline needs, he knew—yet there was something about their unconscious heroism that put a lump in his throat. He would be back soon, he promised, he would pray for them often, he would think of them constantly, and the huge wheels of the ambulance began to creak and to turn, the mules felt the sting of the whip, they plunged into Tongue River, and the Ursuline Mission among the wild Cheyennes was founded.

The children came in crowds and took their seats on the benches that morning and, little by little, they were induced to put on the "white man's clothes" and to learn to read in the white man's primer. But, let a word or a look offend them, these wild little ones of nature would dart out of the door or window, run to the river, pull off their clothing, and throw it back at the dignified and astonished Mother Ignatius, saying: "There, we don't want your old white man's clothes." Oh! for the discipline of Toledo's stately halls. And what could she do, but turn back to the cabin, laugh to herself, and begin all over again. Yes, begin over again, for the parents would whip the runaways, and bring them back to school until they gradually began to love it.

Another parting loomed up now, for the Bishop had ordered Mother back to Miles City "as soon as possible," where a call for another mission awaited her. And the nuns looked at her and at one another with those smiles of ineffable hope, and forgetfulness of self, smiles which no musician has ever sung, no poet has translated into speech, no painter has fixed on canvas. Mother Amadeus was going. Oh! This was April 14th. She took for her companion, Hayewotse (Yellow Stocking) the daughter of White Bull, the great chief of the tribe, the child glad to go wherever Mother went, and promising to return to the Tongue River school only on one condition, that the nuns would give her, upon her return, a little camp stool which had taken the fancy of the little Indian lassie. This little stool was the key to a treasure, the treasure of the Indians' good will, for all wished their children to remain where the daughter of the chief was. Mother's wisdom in treating the Indians, young and old, somewhat like favored children, was the secret of her great success. She always met them half way, and yielded where no principle was at stake. The gift of a tiny chair was the first of many.

What was it in this saintly woman that taught her to deal as successfully with the wild Cheyennes as she had with her cultured Toledo entourage? Who told her to meet these overgrown children of the prairies half way, with reward and encouragement and conciliation? Was it natural magnetism that drew all hearts to her? Was it the radiance of goodness and sincerity that wins even the child at the breast? Was it the divine vocation? At all events, Mother Amadeus of the Heart of Jesus left her nuns, as an heirloom, the tradition of endless patience and maternal gentleness, of untiring energy, forethought, and unselfishness that has made her missions take root and endure, whilst garnering rich harvests of souls. Her spiritual director has written of her: "What can I say of Mother that is not already known to you? I cannot say anything about her before her coming to Montana, and from that time on you have been with her, and so no one better than you could observe her mode of life. Yet I would suggest these points. Her great confidence in Providence and in the protection of St. Joseph in undertaking the establishment of so many missions without having any means at her command. A truly maternal love for the Indian children, for whose welfare she gladly went through every sacrifice and privation. Love, which manifested itself in a sublime manner, especially at times of sickness, when she would spare no pain, nor expense for their relief, and would, as an affectionate mother, gladly watch them all night long. This love for the salvation of the Indians made her always ready to send the nuns to take charge of new missions, though she had hardly subjects enough to carry out the work in the missions already established. And the confidence she had in God's Providence has been well repaid, as the missions where the Ursulines are, in my opinion, are the best in the mountains.

"How she loved the Sacred Heart, the Blessed Virgin, and St. Joseph! How patiently she bore her sufferings and crosses and so resigned in them all. How she cherished her Sisters. These are some of the things I have to say about Mother."

The mission life had begun, the strenuous mission life. Jesus, the all beautiful, was its source; Mother Amadeus of the Heart of Jesus and Bishop Brondel were its channel.

Before leaving the Tongue River country, Mother Amadeus traced the plan for the convent at St. Labre's, and Bishop Brondel, going East, collected the necessary funds for its erection. This first convent was of frame, painted white with the shutters green. It smiled down upon the blowing alfalfa in spring and summer, and upon the glistening snow in winter. The little building was known to all the Indians as the "White House."

"This is our house," Chief White Hawk says. "We built it with our hands. We show it to the Crows when they come to visit us, saying: 'Behold our school! See our little ones, learning the speech and the prayer of the "Weo" (White Man), the Makehahehonawihona with her Wihonas (the nuns) is our true friend. When all abandoned us, and we were alone, she stood in our midst, like a beautiful palm tree in a desolate waste. What she says is true. We trust her.'"

Among the trials of the nuns at St. Labre's, we chronicle the following:

At the turning of the old coach road, in the spring of 1892, was murdered, by the Indians, one John Ferguson. Embarrassed and awed by his silent burden, the murderer hailed Johnnie, a bright lad from our school, who chanced by, singing as was his wont, and challenged him, by all that is sacred in Indian friendship, to help him bury his victim. The Indian code of honor forbade Johnnie to refuse this help to one of his tribe. Both were caught in the act, and both threatened with imprisonment and death. They escaped, however, fled to the mountains, where they were hidden by the faithful fellows of their blood, nor did one betray the secret of their hiding place. The United States soldiers scoured the hills for months in quest of the fugitives. Johnnie and his companion, however, grew weary of this scant and dangerous existence, and urged by the Indian love of valor and bravery, according to their limited knowledge and ideas, they sent word to the United States

Indian agent, that on a given day, at a given hour, they would appear on a given hill near the Rosebud, and that there they would await the fire of the United States troops. I blush to record this triumph of barbarism, but at the appointed hour, as the six riflemen detailed to deal the blow of justice, stood expectant at the foot of the hill, our poor Johnnie and his companion, arrayed in Indian splendor, dancing and singing their proud death dance, appeared, were fired at, and dropped in all the triumph of Indian valor.

Of course, they were hailed as heroes by the tribe, but the nuns mourned the bright boy who, despite his high spirit, had given promise of a better end. The Indians and the white settlers flew to arms, and there was much bloodshed.

Again in the early April of 1897, one John Hoover, who was herding sheep for Mr. Barringer, disappeared. The boy was a cripple, very timid by nature, and mortally afraid of the Indians. His life was a lonely one. For the sheep-herder follows his bleating fold wherever it may stray, keeping away the coyote by day and hastily gathering it into the shed at night and at the approach of the storm. His sole companion is his dog, and, if he be intellectual, his book. Throughout the summer season, he never sees a human countenance, save that of the ranch boy, appointed to bring him twice a month a fresh supply of provisions. The loneliness of the prairie, the dull thud and bleat of his charge, is a strain upon the mind of the poor herder, and many have been known to give way under the pressure, and to assume much of the dullness and heaviness of the sheep.

One Saturday night, John Hoover came into town,

St. Peter's Mission, Montana.

and said to his employer that he believed he would give up the life; his fear of the Cheyennes did but grow— the warning of approaching death. But he was urged to continue still a little longer, and off he started, poor, harmless boy! Farewell!

In a few days afterwards, the sheep came straggling home, without the shepherd, without the dog. Mr. Barringer started off in quest of John Hoover. Reaching the sheep camp, he found all in order, and a pot of beans, not yet soured, on the ashes of the boy's last camp fire. But his search for the herder proved fruitless. Bands of riders scoured the country until, at last, being informed by a wily old Indian, "Makstea" (Square Head), that Hoover had lost his dog, a blooded animal worth seventy-five dollars, and had run home to Wisconsin for fear of his employer, they abandoned the search, and agreed to believe Makstea's story.

But the mortal part of poor John Hoover stretched out on the hillside, under the sleepless eye of God, called aloud for just revenge. And, at length, about a month afterward, the little crippled corpse, its arms extended in the form of a cross, the poor frame pierced with bullets, the dog lying lifeless beside it, was found by a party of riders who were looking for horses.

Active search for the murderers began, and four of our Indians, Philip Stanley, Spotted Hawk, Little Whirlwind, and the boy, Histazio (Shoulder Blade), were arrested and conveyed to Miles City jail. Again Custer County was on fire. The men saw the women safe into Miles City, armed to the teeth, and setting to work to throw up intrenchments and build forts about their ranches, organized into a company of militia for the common defense.

Indian eloquence blossomed out into such speeches as this: "Never were we better prepared for war. We know more than we did in the days of the buffalo. Our braves are braver than the 'Pale Faces.' Let us defend our rights." One "Porcupine's" influence on the religious feeling of his people, began to make itself felt, and his promise of a Cheyenne Messiah and the return of the buffalo seemed to them on the point of realization, the more as the escape of a few of these animals from the Government Bison Range, just at this time gave color to Porcupine's promise, and the buffalo to the Indian is what a lead in a gold mine is to the weary prospector. So the Cheyennes were thoroughly excited, and it really was an hour of danger. The four Ursulines were the only white women on Tongue River, and yet the sweet religious life flowed peacefully on, despite the shouts of the Indians and the firing of the white settlers. But the Ursulines felt no fear, God bless them! They knew the Cheyennes, and the Cheyennes had said: "We shall kill every white man, but we shall not touch the 'White House.'" The squaws fled to the White House for protection, and placed all the children in the school. So that the nuns never were so busy, and on every one of those fearful nights, they went about, from bed to bed, to see little copper faces smiling up to them from snowy pillows, whilst the squaws sought shelter in the wash house, the coal shed, and out upon the porch, for there was not a vacant corner in the house. Colonel Bates, Commanding Officer of Fort Keogh, who afterwards rose to the rank of Brigadier General for his bravery in the Spanish War, actually went all the way out to our mission to see if the Ursulines really had remained at the post of danger. But the thought of fear

had not come near them. Mother's heart was riven to
see her children in so sorry a plight, and she hastened
to their side. "Stanley" and "Histazio" had given testimony against "Spotted Hawk," who lay in Miles City
jail under sentence of death, but to Mother, who hastened to his side to comfort him, he replied, with characteristic Indian imperturbability: "God will not let me
hang, Mother, for I did not kill the white man." And
God stirred the sympathy of the "Indian Rights Association" in Washington, to come down to Miles City to
prove his innocence, which was further and fully confirmed by Stanley's dying confession that he alone had
killed John Hoover.

And the "White House," a glistening pearl in a bed
of emerald, continued to smile peacefully down on the
warlike Cheyenne tribe.

In 1897, the Rev. Jesuit Fathers, who had so long
and so faithfully ministered to the needs at St. Labre's
Mission, were recalled by their Provincial and sent to
other fields of labor. Rev. A. Van der Velden, S.J.,
had grown old in the love and service of the Cheyennes.
He had mastered their very difficult language, and had
watched, for years, over the growth and progress of the
children in the school. He had blessed the Christian
marriages, baptized the children, and was the champion of the Indians' interests on all occasions, whilst
leading a life of solitude, of study, of poverty, of penance and prayer. When the order came, and Father
Van der Velden heard that he really must leave his
dear Cheyennes, in their extreme need, just when the
toil and the sorrows of years seemed on the point of
yielding a rich harvest for heaven, his apostolic heart
well-nigh gave way. He went about, more dead than

alive, offering to God this last supreme sacrifice for the conversion of his beloved Cheyennes.

It is surprising how the saints cling to poverty and privation. At length, the fatal hour came. Father Van der Velden was almost lifted into the buggy. The missionary gave his last blessing. A creaking of wheels, a cloud of dust, and the Jesuits were gone forever from the first Ursuline Indian mission.

Mother Amadeus, however, was there to comfort and direct the nuns in this most painful hour. The priest was gone. Her eloquence and her promise that she would spare no expense or trouble to have a priest ere long, had saved to them the Most Blessed Sacrament, one of the many striking evidences of Our Lord's wonderful response to her exquisite and tender love for Him in the Tabernacle. We shall find many of these evidences as her sainted life wears on. Her early First Communion, her hours before the Cleveland Monstrance, His offer to escape in her arms from the Miles City flood. No wonder her virginal heart was strong for the hours of sacrifice!

The Blessed Sacrament remained behind those folding doors that cut the chapel off from the tiny parlor. How we strove to make up by the fervor of our humble prayer for the absence of the august Sacrifice! Mother Amadeus organized the Perpetual Adoration before the closed and silent door. Every half hour, one of the nuns knelt very close to it with a new responsibility added to the old love. We had become Its guardians. It was a sweet, an awful trust. In the meantime, we were busy cleaning the church and the Fathers' house, and getting them ready for the unknown successor. We clung very close to one another, in a sort of loving

consciousness of our helplessness, our inability to ab-
solve one another from the slightest sin, and hence we
felt a great tenderness and commiseration. On ration
weeks, we were quite alone, for our Indians were at
the Rosebud with their children; the village and the
dance house were deserted, the bell, a sluggard, hung
motionless on the church roof, the windmill scarce
moved its gaunt arms, the alfalfa barely nodded. It
was very warm. Deep silence and solitude reigned,
such as we afterwards knew in Alaska, when the sea
and the river sleep for eight months in the arms of the
ice.

Mother St. Thecla, one of our Mother's dearest children, spent her hours of leisure alone with our revered
Foundress, sunning her missionary soul in the greater
warmth.

August 23d, the anniversary of Mother Amadeus'
profession, dawned during this cruel period of fast
and privation. Still the ardently expected priest had
not arrived. He had, however, written that we might
expect him. So there was a shadow of a foundation
for the exquisite hope in her heart that she would have
Mass, or at least Holy Communion, on that most sacred
anniversary. The hours passed, however, in silent
sameness, as Mother Amadeus knelt upright—a seraph
before the tabernacle, renewing her vows and inviting
the Divine Guest into her heart. Not a sound upon
the river, not a cloud of dust upon the road, not a drop
of water upon her parched and burning lips. We were
awed by the example, such an example as you read
of in the lives of the saints. We almost expected that
an angel would come and lay the silent Whiteness
upon Mother Amadeus' heart.

At last, at 4 P. M., all hope of the arrival waned; we entered the chapel and gently bending her still undaunted will, we lifted more than led her to bed. Prudently and slowly we fed her a little lemon juice through a tube, and then, little by little, her temperature, which was below normal, returned, and we were able to give her a little nourishment. All the while she was so bright and cheerful that the thermometer alone told us her danger. She had had a great feast of love for her anniversary, and her will had proved itself immune against all danger and weakness that flesh is heir to.

Very soon the chaplain alighted from the coach, and for an hour the gleeful bell told the glad tidings to the village. A priest! A priest! No word can repeat the gladness of that bell. We were to have Mass and the Sacraments, and the thought gave wings to our hands and feet in waiting on the "Ambassador of Christ." His personality had vanished. Christ alone, the Good Samaritan, remained. Even the Indians felt this, and expressed it in their untutored, poetic way.

CHAPTER X

THE NOVITIATE

UPON her return to Miles City, April 16, 1884, Mother Amadeus found everything prosperous. She had not recovered from the fatigues of her arduous first journey into the Tongue River Country, when she received a letter from the Jesuit Fathers at St. Peter's, and from the Bishop, telling her to hasten to open, in their rugged fastness, the Novitiate for the Ursulines of Montana.

The first missionary journey had been replete with privations; Mother Amadeus never snatched more than three or four hours' sleep from her nights of suffering and anxious planning for the success of the missions. The poison that had been accidentally administered in Toledo, caused her frequent and most distressing vomiting. Yet what was this? Only personal suffering! So she rose and went to Helena. Two young ladies had been received as novices, two more as postulants, and with these four companions, Mother Amadeus started to open her Novitiate. In Helena, they took seats in the stage to the Bird Tail divide, sixty-nine miles East, for there was no railroad then, and it was St. Peter's Mission that subsequently made the town of Cascade. Those were the pioneer days, when if a woman in Sullivan Valley wanted a needle or a spool of thread, she had to send sixty-nine miles by coach to Helena to get it.

Like a diamond dropped from an eyrie, by an eagle

in its flight, is the little town of Helena, the "Last Chance" of the miners. It sits today in brilliant culture, in the main range of the Rockies, just west of the majestic "Gate of the Mountains." This ponderous portal is not made by the hand of man, but by the headwaters of the Missouri, as they dash down in their journey to St. Louis and the Mississippi. The first sight of the Rocky Mountains makes an indelible impression on every traveler. Here were five missionaries, threading their way through most beautiful gorges, refreshing their souls in the gurgle of the mountain torrent, the soughing of the pine trees, the elevating spectacle of the clouds and the snow-caps so entangled that often they could not tell them apart. Nor were these scenes of sublime peace beneath the shadow of the Bear Tooth, without their tragic memories, for the travelers rested in the cañon of the Little Prickly Pear, and prayed at the grave of Malcolm Clarke,[1] the last white man murdered by the Blackfeet. The account of this tragedy by his daughter, the distinguished educator and writer, Miss Helen P. Clarke, had deeply stirred the heart of Mother Amadeus.

Two days more and our missionaries entered the

[1] While on a tour of inspection through the West during the year of 1877, at which time he was Commander-in-Chief of the Army of the United States, General William T. Sherman stopped over in Helena to rest from the fatigues of a trip through the Yellowstone National Park, during the course of which he had barely escaped being captured by the Nez Percé Indians. Here he met certain of the wounded members of Colonel John Gibbon's command, the gallant Seventh Infantry, who were returning from their hard-fought battle of August 9th on the Big Hole, and had halted at this point to recuperate before passing on to Fort Shaw, their station.

Upon leaving Helena, General Sherman and staff turned northward, and stopped for the night at the ranch of Hon. James Fergus, who was then living at this, the southern, end of the Little Prickly Pear Cañon, in Lewis and Clarke County. After supper, the General strolled about rolling Sullivan Valley, and looked down upon the placid beauty of St. Peter's Mission. Nature in fantastic mood, had long been working her mighty erosion here. Square Butte lay just ahead in dreamy purple, uplifting, silent, majestic, the apex of a giant triangle with the "Crown" and the "Bird Tail" proudly returning its look of recognition. It seemed as though some demi-god, in the long ago, had flung these sentinels there, to guard the historic battle ground of the Blackfeet and the Flatheads, holding it for those heroes of sanctity, Mother Amadeus and the Jesuits.

The spot is singularly noble and beautiful, fit indeed for the battlefield where souls of little children are saved. A few hardy pioneers had settled there, the most noted being Thomas Moran and Edward Lewis, who lent a helping hand whenever and wherever the glory of God demanded it. Above all, there was the church, built by the Jesuit Fathers, and a series of cabins they had sanctified by their first labors. But Father Joseph Damiani, S.J., realizing that "a mission without the Sisters, is no mission at all," had applied to Bishop Brondel, through Father Imoda, S.J., the Vicar General, begging for Mother Amadeus and her nuns, hence the order. Now she was here look-

the place and discovered a grave near by, which he proceeded to investigate. Upon returning to the ranch, he mentioned the occurrence and asked a number of questions in order to fix with certainty the personality of the dead, who was none other than Malcolm Clarke, of whom General Sherman said, in substance, that he well remembered Malcolm Clarke, who had been a fellow cadet with him at West Point and a great favorite there, whom he had then known as a remarkably bright, open-hearted, and high-spirited young man, and for whom he had always prophesied a brilliant future; that he had often scanned reports of operations during the war of the rebellion with the idea in his mind that he might see the name of Malcolm Clarke in connection with some heroic and dashing enterprise; and, finally, that he had lost all trace of his schoolmate since their life at West Point until the discovery by him of this sepulchre among the solitudes of the Rocky Mountains.—W. E. S.

ing down, this dreamy October 30th, in the year of
Our Lord 1884, upon those gorgeous buttes, these tiny
cabins, so poor and yet so holy. In less than a year
since her departure from Toledo, she had erected three
missions, and the magnitude of her work suddenly
filled her with apprehension. There she was alone,
with two young novices, two young postulants, leaning
their inexperience upon her experience, and the work
growing beyond all reckoning, all anticipation. It was
pathetic. But as she looked at the graceful antelopes
out upon the distant butte, as she saw the migratory
birds making themselves ready for flight, she remembered that

> There is a power whose care
> Teaches thy way along the pathless coast
> The desert and illimitable air,
> Lone wandering, but not lost.
> He Who from zone to zone
> Guides through the boundless sky thy certain flight,
> In the long way that I must tread alone
> Will lead my steps aright,

and she alighted from the coach, her queenly smile of
trust reigning once more, to greet the Rev. Jesuit
Fathers, and Messrs. Moran and Lewis, as they stood
at the door of the mission church to welcome her.
"Skull Butte" rose, seemingly at a stone's throw before her, and the Fathers told her that it was named
from the many skulls of the Blackfeet and the Flatheads found there, and how once, when these two
fierce tribes were lined up ready for a deadly en-
counter, Father de Smet had stepped unarmed between
them, and raising his hand and his voice, had disarmed those ancestral foes. Turning their heads to

the left, they beheld another butte, its summit cloven
with a gigantic "U," and Father Damiani at once
named the butte "Ursula," and the rock at its base,
where bubbles a perennial spring of crystal water, he
called, with equal symbolism and poetry, "Amadeus."

Stretching east and west, beneath the polar star,
was another little line of cabins, four of these, twelve
feet by twenty feet, connected by an exterior porch in
the consecrated form of mission architecture as we
admire it still at St. Francis Solano, San Rafael, and
Santa Clara, California, those typical missions of our
country. They sheltered in the angle where they met,
the church, the bell tower. From within, the many-
tongued throat of the old bell, called out the signal for
rising in the early morning, the Angelus, three times a
day, and Holy Mass on Sundays and feast days, until
the hills and the valley burst into a loud chorus of
echoes.

The cabins had been the residence of the Fathers,
but they vacated them for the nuns, who thus found
themselves, each one, with a room to herself. That
night the Fathers invited the nuns over to supper in
their new residence. We shall not say what they had.
There had been an attempt "á la man" at a banquet.
The nuns saw something very brown they mistook for
fruitcake. As others partook unstintingly, they ventured to partake. Alas! it was bread, bread of ecclesiastical baking! The next morning, one of the novices was formally installed as mission baker, and
Mother Amadeus sent over to the delighted Fathers
some bread of fleecy whiteness.

And so the sweet mission life began in joy, in
trust, in incessant activity. But it had not lasted

long, when the delicate frame of the Foundress gave way. She was attacked by pneumonia, and she lay stretched on the floor of her little cabin to receive Extreme Unction.

The devil does try to defeat great works in their incipiency. The four young novices stood about aghast, but Father Damiani knew what to do, and he did it. From Fort Shaw came at once the military doctor, and soon, too, Mother Stanislaus, whom he had called by dispatch. This devoted friend stood at Mother Amadeus' bedside and soon nursed her back to health. She told her that she had come to take her and her four companions back to Toledo, where all were most anxious to have her. Her pleading was in vain. It broke like the waves of the sea against the rock of Mother Amadeus' sublime vocation. *"Heko et hamsto,"* our Indians say; "I stand firm like the mountains" that "shakes not its top for any blast that blows."

Upon hearing of Mother Amadeus' illness, Bishop Brondel had telegraphed to Mother St. Frances, then stationed at Miles City, to hasten to St. Peter's, and to do all in her power to save the precious life. "You may travel alone," the Bishop wired, "for you will find Archbishop Seghers on the west-bound train. He will be your companion."

The great Archbishop-Martyr talked that night with our sweet "Violet of the Rockies." One of the questions he asked, was: "Can I obtain Mother and the Ursulines for Alaska?" Mother Amadeus' illness alone prevented his going to St. Peter's. He was forging ahead to martyrdom. She lay stretched on the floor of the cabin struggling with death. Unsearchable

Providence of God! These were twin-born souls, yet their ships passed in the night. They met not here below. But Mother Amadeus felt him beckoning, and it was a consolation to her to know that he had asked for her, and she felt he would bring her, as he did, to Alaska in the end.

As Mother Amadeus began to convalesce, Father Damiani was there to check and regulate the austerity of the future "Theresa of Alaska." Henceforth, she was to have a bed, and she was to occupy the little sheltered cabin that served as sacristy. A little space was partitioned off, just wide enough to admit an iron bed six feet by twenty-five inches, with standing room beside it, and night and day, when the curtain was drawn, she should look through a tiny window into the sanctuary, see the little red light, and the statue of Our Lady that Father de Smet had left there.

Mother Stanislaus left the Montana community many tokens of her generous love, and a mighty helper in the person of Mary Fields. Mary Fields was a colored woman, strong as a man, who remembered slavery, and who had been a confidential servant in the house of Judge Dunne, Mother Amadeus' oldest brother. When Mrs. Dunne died, she had brought the children from Florida to Toledo, where Mother Amadeus was Superior, and she remained there. When the news of Mother Amadeus' illness reached Toledo, she followed Mother Stanislaus out West. She loved Mother with the devotion of her race, and she elected to live and die at St. Peter's Mission.

The five nuns, aided by Mary, began the mission life once more. Soon new helpers came, and it was high time.

Father F. Eberschweiler, S.J., the chaplain of the Toledo convent, Mother Amadeus' great helper when first she became Superior, had preceded her into the Rocky Mountain missions. He had opened a mission for the Gros Ventre and Assiniboine Indians in the Little Rockies and Bear Paw Mountains. Whilst he was preparing for a school of his own, he sent Mother Amadeus a priceless gift: a wagon load of Indian girls from the Milk River country. Agessa, daughter of Chief Bushy Head; Watzinitha, Eyahe's daughter, and Atathan, granddaughter of Akipinaki, were the leaders of the band. Together, in the ponderous wagon, they began their lifelong friendship, together they lived their little lives at St. Peter's Mission, together they learned from Mother Amadeus to love Jesus, Mary, and Joseph, and together they died in her loving arms, little virgins consecrated to God. The arrival of the wagon from the Bear Paw was an event indeed. These were the first children of the dear mission, and in order to receive and educate them, Mother Amadeus had called to her side two of her most devoted companions, Mother St. Francis, "the humble violet of the Rockies," and her dear Mother Mary of the Angels.

The Queen of Sheba received no greater welcome at the hands of Solomon, than did Agessa, Watzinitha, Atathan, and their companions from Mother Amadeus and the Ursulines of St. Peter's. Arrayed in white aprons and sleeves, two combs and a brush in each nun's pocket, they advanced to meet the newcomers. Mother Amadeus enfolded each child in her maternal arms, whilst the wondrous smile of her eye and lip won and subjugated the trembling, wild little hearts beneath the buckskin, and sunned away the first tears of lonesomeness and shyness.

First the children must eat, yes, abundantly, and then they must take their stand behind the cabins in a spot secluded from view, where basin, towels, soap, and tubs of water had been provided. And then began the missionary's greatest crucifixion, for each one of those star-eyed darlings was a legion. The long black locks might by no means be cut off, which would have been the simplest and the quickest way. Pearls came crackling off the combs and fell into basins of coal oil. Then the wee lassies must taste soap and water, and put on white man's clothing, and know the strange, sweet comfort of living henceforth, each one alone in her new, clean garments. Mother St. Francis has left a graphic account of this first solemn ceremony of initiation, since then so often, so often repeated, and without which no Indian child may be introduced into the spotless dormitory.

"Dear Sister," Mother St. Francis writes, "in answer to your question about our dearest Mother, how I wish I were able to give you some facts descriptive of our early days, but I am not able to gather but what you already know: Mother's Christlike charity and love for the poorest of the poor. The neglected Indians seemed to be her all, her first thought in beginning our missionary work in Montana.

"I can yet see when the little Gros Ventre were brought to St. Peter's, their heads alive with vermin. Mother was the first to begin the search with her delicate nature, and she always suffered from nausea and stomach trouble ever after the poisoning in Toledo. She was smiling and already at work when I came with

my comb in hand and she said to me: 'Don't forget to
form your intention,' and at the same time she made
the sign of the cross.   This thought inspired me very
much at the time and encouraged me on with the re-
pugnant work which was carried on out of doors behind
the cabins.   Dear Mother used to laugh and say: 'Sister,
mine seem to fly off the comb, do yours?   It is hard
to catch them.'

"We had a basin with coal oil where we deposited
our live-stock, and where they did not thrive long."

St. Peter's Mission had been visited by Father de
Smet, and Father Point as far back as 1841, but it was
not until 1858 that it was formally opened by Fathers
Hoecken and Imoda, and Brother Magri.   Closed for
awhile in 1860, because of the hostilities of the Blackfeet and the Flatheads, it was re-opened in 1861 by
Fathers Imoda and Giorda and Brother Francis.   Father
Imoda later called to his assistance the young Roman
who succeeded him as Superior when he himself became Vicar General of the Diocese of Helena.

Born in Rome, Father Joseph Damiani early entered
the ranks of the Society of Jesus.   His first efforts were
spent at the "Collegio Massimo" where, with his fellow
novice, the Prince of that Patrician name he distinguished himself as a teacher by his clear and cultured
mind, his noble uprightness, his zeal for the salvation of
souls.   To avoid the honors for which these qualities
marked him out, he asked to join the devoted band laboring in the Rocky Mountains.   If the sacrifice of home
and Fatherland is always heroic, it is doubly so in *"un
vero Romano di Roma,"* who seldom consents to leave
the mystic circle of the "Seven Hills."   It was Father Damiani as Superior of St. Peter's Mission, who   came

RT. REV. LOUIS FRANÇOIS LAFLÈCHE, BISHOP OF THREE RIVERS.
THE CHRYSOSTOM OF CANADA.

forward to greet Mother Amadeus on the evening of October 30, 1884. He was the friend whom a kind and watchful Providence placed at her side, and verily and long did he prove such.

The mission took root and prospered. More helpers came, and ere long, Mother Amadeus was enabled to put up a stone building whose reposeful and artistic beauty was a joy to look upon. When the men dug the cornerstone of the building out of the quarry at Square Battle, they found beneath it thirty rattlesnakes, and in their own native poetry, they said this was symbolic of the evil Mother had already driven out of the country. In 1913 she went with Natzinitha and one Ursuline companion on a quest for helpers, and returned from the East with seventeen young ladies, besides six professed nuns lent her for three years by the old Ursuline Monasteries of Quebec and Three Rivers. Escorted by her distinguished brother, Judge Dunne, she visited President Cleveland at the White House, Cardinal Satolli in Washington and Cardinal Gibbons in Baltimore, and was received with distinguished honor by Princess Eulalia who had come to represent her brother, the King of Spain, at the Chicago Exposition. In the old monasteries of Canada she was received with open arms. Bishop Laflèche of Three Rivers was the Missionary "by excellence." In 1846 he had been sent by Bishop Provencher of St. Boniface up into the wilds of what is now the Vicariate Apostolic of Keewatin. He elected for his residence an icy spot, La Cross Island, which he made the first parish of the extreme North, a parish as big as the whole of France, through which wandered two thousand restless Crees. Here, with those first wonderful Oblates of Mary Immaculate, afterwards Archbishop Taché of St. Boniface and Bishops Grandin and Faraud of St. Albert and Athabasca-Mackenzie, he lived the Mission life in all its ideal beauty, its deep peace and joy. "Long live the North," these four great men kept exclaiming!" *"Moloc a bu."*

Alas! in 1848 the iron chain of obedience dragged Father Laflèche from his earthly paradise to make him Bishop of Three Rivers. All the dear past came flooding back to his heart when he beheld Mother Amadeus. He understood at once. He read her big heart! Yes, of course, Mother Amadeus of the Heart of Jesus should have the help of his Ursulines.

And the old Missionary bell of his episcopal city, rang her coming as she drove up to the portal. The community was assembled in the Chapter room to give her solemn welcome, and many generous co-workers offered themselves to follow her back to Montana. Three were lent, and these joyously followed her the next day as she went back to New York. In Quebec they clung to her with exquisite tenderness, for they remembered her visit in 1877; they too lent her three professed nuns, a most unusual concession in this strictly cloistered community. These six professed nuns were an invaluable help whilst the Montana novices were getting their training, and we cannot be grateful enough to our sisters in Canada for this generous gift. Unstintingly did they spend themselves for the good of our poor Indian children whilst they labored in our midst.

Gratitude arises from the pure heart at the bidding of the Holy Spirit. Let ours be theirs, without measure. There are magnetic points in humanity as in nature. Cardinal Bégin and the dear old Bishop of

Three Rivers received our Mother as though she were a second "Mary of the Incarnation." It was soul-stirring for us poor missionaries, little used as we were in our incessant toil and struggle for existence, to the amenities of life, to see the deep-seated esteem of the people and their chief Pastors for our Order in truly Catholic Canada.

CHAPTER XI

MORE HELPERS—MORE MISSIONS

FATHER FREDERICK EBERSCHWEILER had settled in the Milk River country at the foot of the "Little Rockies" over against the "Bear Paw." These mountains are full of might and majesty, frowning up to a blue, blue sky, which doubtless whispered their name to the poetic and observant Indians. The "Little Rockies" are so rich in woods and waters, so full of natural wonders, gorges, cañons, glens and bridges of rock that they suggest the name of "The Paradise Lost of the Indians." Here Father Eberschweiler, the distinguished poet and musician, had opened a Mission for the Gros Ventre and Assiniboine tribes forty-five miles southeast of the Milk River.

The two tribes united by friendship, intermarriage and a certain harmony of mutual intercourse, as a gentle nature—the Gros Ventre—will link with a stronger, the Assiniboine, or "Rock Sioux." These Indians had been attracted to this beautiful locality from Mexico, by the pleasures of the chase. They had been visited by Fathers de Smet, Point, Giorda, Rappagliosi, Grassi, Damiani, and Joseph Bandini, but the Mission was not founded until Father Eberschweiler settled there in 1885. It was from this site that Mother Amadeus's great missionary friend had sent her, as we have seen, her first Indian girls: Agessa, Atathan, Watzinitha, and, when all was ready for his own school, he obtained Mother St. Francis as the first local Superior to open it. The ceremony of formal opening took place on September 14th, the "Exaltation of the Holy Cross," in 1887, and the Mission was called St. Paul's. Many lovely girls were here civilized and educated. Mechtilde, among many others, sanctified herself there, and thence went to St. Peter's, where she died almost in the fame of sanctity. Volumes might be written of this Mission alone. It was an oasis of peace, and Mother Amadeus often went there for rest and spiritual joy. God seemed to speak very loud to His simple children of the "Little Rockies" and echoes of the supernatural were not infrequent.

St. Francis Xavier Mission was opened a few days after St. Paul's on October 2, 1887, feast of the Holy Angels. The great apostle of this Mission among the Crows was the Rev. Father Peter Paul Prando, who died in July, 1906, but the tribe was first visited by Father Barcelo. The Crow Tribe, the largest in the United States, is a powerful and intelligent one. Their name "Absarki" seems to point to a Mexican origin, as it is the name of a bird found in Mexico alone, and nowhere in the Rockies. Father de Smet, who gave the Crows their first notions of Christianity, says of them: "This race is one of the noblest in the desert. They are tall, robust, well formed, have a piercing eye, an aquiline nose and teeth of ivory whiteness. While superior to the other tribes by their intelligence, they surpass them also in their superstitious notions and ceremonies."

"Iron Bull," the Codrus of this race, whom no one was deemed fit to succeed in the chiefdom, gives the following graphic account of the creation:

"I, Iron Bull, knew my father. My father knew his father, and so it was for seven generation. Before that only 'Old Wolf' (God in Crow), the great spirit, was living, and the earth was so small that there was only room enough for 'Old Wolf' to sit down. All around the earth were the great waters. Now it came to pass that "Old Wolf" one day took earth and threw it into the water, and the first Crow Indian was thus formed. This Crow was blind and could not open his mouth, so 'Old Wolf' called into existence the buffalo, the elk and the other animals. He also made more Crows, both male and female, by throwing more earth into the water. Then the land was too small for the newly made inhabitants. So 'Old Wolf' called for a bird and sent it under the water, and as the bird did not return, he sent another after it which came to the surface with mud in his beak with which 'Old Wolf' made much land, and then he made the Piegans, the Sioux, the Snakes and many other tribes, and placed them in different parts of the circle he drew. But he located the Crows in the middle because they are the first people in the world. They have always been at war with the other Indians, and they have never been vanquished, but they have killed all their enemies, and taken many scalps."

Thus we find our people trailing memories of the Mosaic record into their proud national traditions, and giving unconscious testimony to the existence of one sole God and Creator, a truth which is written deep even in the most untutored heart. The warlike spirit of the Crows was by no means dead when Mother Amadeus went to them.

"Swordbearer" proclaimed himself the Crow Messiah, and went about with a certain powder which, he boasted, made him and his followers invulnerable. They could therefore exterminate the Whites. The valley of the Big Horn was aflame when the Ursulines reached the Agency. The Indians surrounded the fort in battle array, and bright in war paint and feathers. Major Armstrong, the Indian Agent, not knowing how to meet this grave emergency, welcomed the Ursulines as messengers of Peace. He begged Mother Amadeus to quiet the Indians. In noble fearlessness, she stepped out onto the platform amid the whizzing arrows, the shot and shell, confronted the painted, howling chiefs, smiling and queenly, this daughter of the martyrs, of the kings of Iregan. Whether it was the chaste and holy attitude and habit, whether it was the courageous bearing, the sunny, trustful smile, the radiant goodness that no heart ever withstood that swayed them we know not. (Mother Amadeus could not then speak Crow.) At all events the Indians stopped firing. Sword-bearer rode up to the agent and said: "We shall not fire while that holy woman is there." And not only did they cease hostilities; they accompanied Mother Amadeus and the nuns in triumph the twenty-three miles that separated them from St. Xavier's Mission, and left their little ones to the hallowed care of the "Virginettas" (the nuns).

CHAPTER XII

A Triology of Danger

WHILST traveling to and fro from the Crow Mission Mother Amadeus encountered three dangers so great, that one alone would have sufficed to dampen courage less heroic. She had left St. Xavier's one day, with her Ursuline companion, one of the Rev. Jesuit Fathers, an Indian boy and the driver, when suddenly one of Montana's famous blizzards set in, and piled up before them massive and impenetrable walls of snow. It was impossible to proceed with their heavy wagon. There was but one thing to do; unhitch the horses and send the Indians on to Fort Custer for help. Night came on, as it does in those blizzards, cold, early, dark and threatening, solitude and silence and the monster stars looking ominously down, with such shelter as the wagon and the snow wall could afford. To know Mother Amadeus you must have seen her in emergencies such at this: the bright eye, nay even the smile of confidence, and the precise word of command that belong to magnetic genius. She spent the night rubbing the hands and feet of her companions, cheering them to keep away the sleep of death, and walking up and down in the deep snow. She prayed, too, to Mary, the Queen of the Ursulines, "Our Lady of the Snow," whom we used to invoke even then, for Alaska was always the goal of our ambition. Can any one count and measure those endless hours? The Holy Angels alone, I think.

The long night wore on, with the dawn came help

from Fort Custer. All were lifted into the Government ambulance, and the penitential vigil was over.

Our Lord watched and prayed upon the mountain and called the stars by name as they arose one by one over the verdant Carmel, the snow-capped Hermon, and the broad rich plain of Esdrelon, to keep him company whilst he prayed. Perhaps our marvelous work was born during this night of Mother Amadeus' contemplation and suffering. It is a mystic picture, a memory full of majesty. Many religious Orders have been founded during the vigils of the saints.

When they reached Fort Custer, legs and arms frozen, the ladies tenderly lifted the Ursulines into baths of coal oil, and then into snowy beds where they were forced to remain three days before they recovered the use of frozen members.

Then again Mother Amadeus was on her way. She was going from St. Labre's to the Crows by the Custer trail over the Wolf Mountains. The Rev. Driver was vaunting the prowess of his steeds. "Nunicaweo" was in high spirits. He had found, at last, a person of his own undaunted spirit to labor for the Cheyennes. The horses, too, seemed in fine spirits, for at the entrance of a wood, they got beyond all control, and made for the verge of an impending precipice. Mother Amadeus' unerring eye saw danger. Throwing ahead the basket of provisions she said: "Jump, Father," and out she went just in time to see the horses dash over the chasm, break the buggy into bits, and throw themselves to a bloody death. The missionaries were safe, but the Crow Mission was still very far away. The brave Mother unhesitatingly lifted the provision basket, and with words of encouragement led the way through the woods. All night they walked weary and footsore, over the crackling snow, and yet her heart was ever light and joyous.

As the gray dawn came creeping over the tree-tops, and they had reached the outskirts of the wood, other figures, too, gray and ghastly, crept on apace, preceded and accompanied by an ominous tramp and thud, that indicated their numbers. The wolves, the hungry winter wolves! They had scented the travelers and their basket of provisions, and they were fearless. Already Mother Amadeus could discern the keen, bright, pitiless eyes; she felt upon her face the angry breath of merciless hunger. She knelt down in the snow, extended her tired wonder-working arms in the form of a cross and began aloud, *"Memorare o piissima Virgo Maria non esse auditum."* Already the thud had grown less distinct, and when Mother Amadeus had finished her prayer, she looked up to see the gray cloud of affrighed monsters swept around the mountain side. Is the age of miracles passed?

Soon again the mighty protecting arm of God was stretched out over Mother Amadeus' miraculous life. She had made her yearly visitation at St. Xavier's Mission and had gone to St. Charles' Mission at the camp of Chief "Plenty Coos" (Many Scalps) on Pryor Creek. She was returning to Billings with her companions. The Brother was following with the wagon for freight. The nuns were in a buggy that had been hired at a livery stable in Billings. The day was clear and very cold. It was the feast of St. Barbara, 1894. The nun's at St. Peter's noticed afterwards that at the very hour when Mother Amadeus was in such great danger, the Most Blessed Sacrament was taking possession of her tiny cell, for the chapel was undergoing repairs and, out of reverence, the nuns had transformed her room into a chapel. Meanwhile the horses were straining their haunches, and pulling lustily over the crisp soil. Blue Creek is an affluent of the Yellowstone. The driver thought he remembered the exact spot of the ford. As they drove along, a mile or so beyond the swollen, noisy torrent, Mother Amadeus noticed a cowboy camp, but she took little notice of the sight so very common in Montana. The detail, scarcely noted then, came back to her in her hour of danger. When they reached Blue Creek, it was swollen beyond record, and the driver was surprised not to see the Government sign, marking the site of the ford, but as he thought he remembered it, and that there would surely be some warning if the danger were what it seemed, he plunged fearlessly into the roaring stream. Scarcely had the horses pulled out from the shore than they stood, trembling and snorting. The water had suddenly risen above the carriage wheels, and reached the waists of the nuns. It was very cold. Huge blocks of ice were floating past, and knocking so violently against the buggy that Mother Amadeus feared that, at any moment, it might be overturned. Some invisible angel held the horses. One step, and all had been plunged to certain death. They stood like steeds of stone, however, only now and again trembling and snorting as though to give warning of danger. Mother Amadeus rose to the level of the dread surroundings. The driver had fainted; the nuns were calling: "Oh, Mother, save us, save us." "I will," she replied, and extending her brave arms in the form of a cross, she promised to erect, in our chapel, a statue of "the Heart of Jesus

pleading." She then roused the driver, scolded him
for his weakness in leaving them thus in danger, bade
him creep carefully over the hind wheels of the buggy,
wade to the shore, detach one of the horses from the
wagon that had followed, and ride to the cowboy camp
for help. This, the only hope of rescue, was most difficult of execution, difficult and dangerous, an imprudent
move would upset the buggy, frighten the horses and
dash them all headlong into the frozen stream. Dispatch, too, was necessary for the frozen waters
were a menace to life. The noble animals, however,
as though conscious of responsibility, stood, with almost
human intelligence, motionless and firm in spite of the
cold, in spite of the blocks of floating ice. The nuns
instinctively clung to Mother Amadeus, as all involun-
tarily pay homage to genius and virtue in the hour of
danger. Three deadly quarters of an hour passed,
interminable and full of anguish, but at length the
help sent for arrived. The brave Montana men, as
tender, as reverent and unselfish as ever made a nation,
climbed cautiously over the back wheels of the buggy
and lifted the nuns one by one! All wanted Mother
Amadeus to leave first. Not she! She used her authority to remain last in that frozen Charybdis. As the
nuns stood upon the shore and watched her standing
alone in the stream, they offered to God their lives in
exchange for hers. At last she, too, was lifted gently
onto the shore. Then they all wept and fell into one
another's arms, and intoned the *Te Deum.*

"There is no wisdom, there is no prudence, there is
no counsel against the Lord." [1]

"Let us sing to the Lord, for He is gloriously magi-

1 Prov. xxi. 30.

fied.   The horse and the rider He hath thrown into the sea." [2]

Clouds of steam rose from their habits as they stood dripping about the fire kindled on the shore.   That night the men slept in the snow, and the nuns slept in the cabin with the cowboys' loaded revolvers under their pillows.

[2] **Ex. xv. 1.**

CHAPTER XIII

NEW JOYS—NEW MISSIONS

THE twenty-third of August, Mother Amadeus' Silver Jubilee, was coming on apace, and the nuns were busy with needle, pencil and brush, making ready to celebrate the twenty-fifth anniversary of her profession. Monsignor Stephan, Director of the Bureau of Indian Missions; Bishop Brondel, Fathers Eberschweiler and Damiani all were there to do honor to the successful Foundress of the Indian Mission.

Corregio has painted the well known picture of the Nativity in which all is poverty and darkness, save one central point, whence radiates all the light. So it was on August 23, 1889, in the log cabin convent at St. Peter's Mission. For few women, I think, comparatively very few, have possessed magnetism, firmness, goodness, to the same extent as Mother Amadeus of the Heart of Jesus. She discovered each one's aptitudes at a glance; she worked not alone, but through each one of us, so that her influence for good emanated through the spheres of each one's activity. She opened hearts and natures the most opposite. Whatever our troubles, our difficulties, we could tell them all to Mother.

We called her "Mother."
Montana called her "The Mother."
The Cheyennes called her "Makemahehonawi-
  hona."
The Blackfeet called her "Ninaki."

The Assiniboines called her "Ethanshayai."

The Gros Ventre called her "Nagathay."

The Kalispel called her "Komenskolinzuten."

The Eskimos called her "Anayakachpak," but all these words in many languages meant the one sweet thing: "Mother."

About this time Mother Katherine Drexel gave Mother Amadeus the princely gift of $5,000 and the priceless gift of her friendship and esteem. The two great women were knit together by a double love; love of the Indian race, love of the Most Blessed Sacrament, and to these two was afterwards joined a third, Mrs. Thomas Fortune Ryan. As Mother Drexel had devoted her fortune to the salvation of the Indian race, Mrs. Ryan gave hers to erect shrines for the Most Blessed Sacrament. Not a watchful red light casts its gleam of hope and joy on the snows of Alaska, but whispers the name of Mrs. Thomas Fortune Ryan.

The year after Mother Amadeus had celebrated the twenty-fifth anniversary of her consecration to God, Our Lord sent her two more Missions. In March 1890, she opened St. Ignatius Mission. This was to be a kindergarten for the children of the Kalispel, the Flatheads and the allied tribes. The Very Rev. Father Cataldo, who was then Superior of the Jesuits of Montana, called upon her for this experiment. He felt that the conversion of those Indians could be best affected by training the little ones from the cradle up, and right glad was Mother Amadeus to plant the banner of St. Ursula in the historic soil of the Bitter Root, the field sanctified by the first labors of the pioneer missionary, Father de Smet.

So Mother Amadeus with a new colony of Ursulines, was soon under way again.

Two passes, McDonald and Priest, cross the continental divide, the great Northern Pacific Railway following the later. Butler, Montana, on account of its position, is called the "Backbone of the Rockies." The railway enters the famous Mullan tunnel, debouching at Blossburg, and wends its way westward over the O'Keefe and Marent trestles, 112 and 226 feet in the air, respectively—this latter the highest in the Northern Pacific system—revealing below a wealth of mountain streams, of luxurious pine trees and fertile valleys. Even a less pure, less poetic soul looking down upon the splendid deep might well be filled with awe, but when soon afterward, the name Ravalli greeted Mother Amadeus' ear, amazement made room for gratitude and love. What a life of heroic and enlightened charity the name Ravalli recalled! Here the travelers exchanged their seats in the railroad for one in the Mission coach, and a ride in the shadow of peak McDonald.

Often on her subsequent visits to St. Ignatius, as she rode from the railroad station to the Mission, Mother Amadeus looked with wondering eyes at the great Bison Range fenced in by the Government in 1890, 18,000 acres enclosed by a strong fence some five or six feet high, where the quondam lords of the prairie roam at large. One of our Indians, Pablo, revived the almost extinct species, and grew so rich that he could lend money to all the white settlers about. He and his friend Allard, raised large herds of buffalo which may still be seen at Ravalli, one of them selling his herd to the Canadian, the other to the United States government. The buffalo had meant so much to the Indians, and for this reason

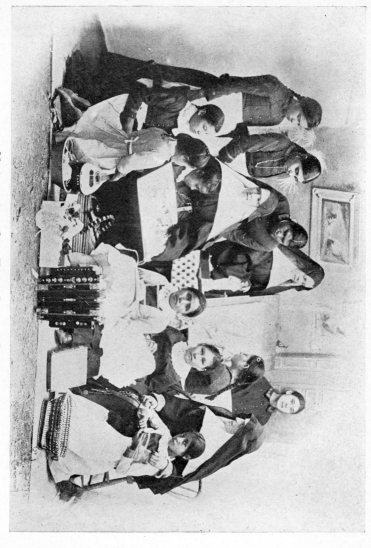

MOTHER AND OUR FIRST INDIAN GIRLS.

they meant so much to Mother Amadeus who looked wonderingly at them as she drove to and from St. Ignatius.

When in 1803, President Jefferson sent a message to Congress asking for an appropriation of $2,500 for an exploration of the Missouri and Colombia Rivers, Captain Lewis and Captain Clark were chosen to lead the expedition. These were the first white men to enter the present limits of the State of Montana.

Old Eugenie, who was still living in 1890, when Mother Amadeus opened the Mission at St. Ignatius, remembered the reverence with which the Indians carried about the first white men they had ever seen, how they wondered at the unseemly trousers, and pityingly gave them blankets to cover their legs before they suffered them to treat with Indian dignitaries. One thing in Flathead history is, I think, unique in the history of pagandom: they themselves asked for the missionaries and sent four deputations to St. Louis to obtain a priest. A band of Iroquois from Caughnawaga, Canada, had found their way down into the Bitter Root country, and had been adopted into the Flathead tribe. "Old Ignace" had been charmed by the virtues of the virgin Kateri Tegakwitha, whose cause is now up for canonization.

So eloquently did he speak to the Flatheads about Kateri and about the labors of the Jesuit missionaries and the beauty of the Church, that they determined to send for the "Black Gowns." About the camp-fires they would sit during the long winter nights, listening to the stories he told, and little by little they determined to go to St. Louis to obtain these teachers of the truth for their people. The journey to St. Louis, which is now accomplished in two days, was at that time a great undertaking, not only because of the wilderness, but chiefly because of hostile tribes. Four young braves offered to go that their people might hear about the "Great Spirit." They reached the distant city, but two of them fell ill and died there. The others, on their return journey, were murdered and never saw their people again. The arrival of these Indians in St. Louis was of course much talked of, and as the Jesuits could not at once respond to the call, two Methodist ministers, with their wives, followed the returning Indians to the meeting place where the Flatheads were awaiting the coming of the "Black Gowns.'' Seeing the ministers they indignantly refused to accept them; the true "Black Gowns," they knew, had had no wives nor did these men wear black gowns. They wore no cross, nor did they offer the "Great Prayer"—(Holy Mass). This was in 1831.

The Flatheads were not discouraged. Ignace offered to go to St. Louis. The Fathers had not then the men to spare for the great work, and Ignace returned to tell the Flatheads that he had indeed seen the "Black Gown," but that they could not come now. Again, a third time, these determined Indians sent to St. Louis, but the party fell in with the Sioux and were killed to a man. Nothing daunted, the brave Flatheads sent a fourth deputation to St. Louis, and this time, 1841, their perseverance was rewarded by the coming of the great Father de Smet.

Does it not present a wonderful and a beautiful picture to see these Indians, seated about their camp-fires, whilst the moon peeps over proud McDonald, and Old Ignace stands erect talking, talking not about war and Blackfeet scalps, but about the spreading St. Lawrence, the chaste and penitent Kateri, and wonderworking "Black Gowns" until their enthusiasm is fired and they expose themselves to the dangers of four most perilous expeditions that they may learn to know and love the "Great Spirit?" Francis Ignace Saxa, who was still living when Mother Amadeus went to St. Ignatius, had been baptized when a boy by Father de Smet in St. Louis. On Father de Smet's second visit, he was accompanied by Fathers Point, Megarino and Menetray and by Brothers Speth, Huet and Classens. The first Mission was founded at "Old St. Mary," now Stevensville, Montana, but was transferred to its present site in 1854 by Father Menetray.

Father de Smet says of the Flatheads that "among them is found the beau ideal of the Indian character uncontaminated by the whites," and Lieutenant Mullan, U. S. A., adds, "the heroism of the Flatheads in battle and their good faith toward others has been the theme of praise by both priest and layman. They are the best Indians in the territory" (of Montana). The confrères of these Indians are the Kootenai, the Nez Percés, Pend d'Oreilles, and the Kalispel, with whom they are associated and allied by sympathy and friendship, intermarriage.

"Carcashee" was the chief when Mother Amadeus opened her Mission. "Charlos" was with his band at the Jocko. "Arlee," the last of the war chiefs, had died, Old Eugenie, who lived to be one hundred years old, gave Mother the tribute of all her untutored love, and admiration. She told that when Lewis and Clark came, they gave the Flatheads a present of a bell and a looking glass. This latter the chief poetically mistook to be the soul. He stored this treasure jealously away in his own "teepee," and when the young girls of the tribe gathered about him on Saturday nights, as they regularly did, being summoned by the bell to keep the weekly vigil and to watch for the rising of the sun on the seventh morning, they were admitted, one by one, to look each at her own soul—*i. e.*, her face in the glass, and when thus purified, by prayer and self-contemplation, they beheld the first streaks of dawn athwart proud McDonald, they rose, joined their hands above their heads, and then prostrated on the ground face downward, and prayed aloud, each one crying out the needs of her soul.

There is something noble in our Indians, even in their poor benighted paganism.

On the day of the opening of the Mission, the Very Rev. Father Cataldo gathered the Flatheads about the great Mission cross and spoke to them, telling them to send their little ones to the Ursulines. The chief woman gave her baby to Mother Amadeus who wrapped it tenderly in her choir mantle, and carried it to the kindergarten. Then Mother went about among the other women and stretched her arms to each one. Not one of them could resist the ineffable maternal attitude, the smile, so beautiful in its trust, its goodness, and the kindergarten was soon full—the first kindergarten ever heard of among the Indians, for never before had an Indian woman trusted her baby to another. Carashee was looking on in silence. "The Father hath spoken well," at last he said, "but the Mother hath spoken better." Mother Amadeus had not opened her lips.

CHAPTER XIV

CHIEF BATTLER DREAMS

Soon after the successful opening of St. Ignatius Mission Mother Amadeus' generous heart was rejoiced by the arrival of fresh helpers. They had come in time. Father Damiani, transferred to the Holy Family among the fierce Blackfeet, called for a colony of Ursulines to teach his school. On August 23, 1890, the anniversary of her profession, Mother Amadeus sent him three. They traveled by coach and reached their destination on the evening of the 25th. It being Saturday night, they remained at the Government Stockade at Piegan. Father Damiani said Mass for them on a piano belonging to the lovely Miss Isabel Clarke, the Matron of the Agency School. She was the daughter of Malcolm Clarke, the friend of General Sherman at West Point, at whose tragic murder in 1870, the litle girl had played so heroic a part. The graceful and beautiful girl had decked her room as a chapel, her piano as an altar and with the Ursulines she received Holy Communion with the fervor of an angel. That afternoon the Ursulines drove over to the home built for them by the generosity of Mother Katherine Drexel.

One little circumstance must be recorded here among the many remembered only by the Angels. As the nuns were leaving the Stockade, Chief Battler desired to speak to them. It was a beautiful, sunny Sunday, and the Ursulines, with their friends and the Rev. Father Damiani, stood in a semicircle before the stalwart Indian. He was wrapped in a summer blanket which he alternately clasped about him or suffered to float in the breeze. "Some years ago," he said in Piegan, "I dreamed a dream. This dream was a medicine. I was weeping. The buffalo had fled, and the glory of the Blackfeet race was forever departed. I wept for the Braves whose bones were blanching on the hillside. But I wept more than all for our little ones growing up about us everywhere, scions and hope of a once proud race, now left without the skill and might of their fathers amid the selfish white race whose knowledge and speech and prayer they know not.

But suddenly there arose before me, three Virgins from the East that came to me upon a cloud one day before the dawn. They gathered the little ones about them and taught them all the secrets that the white man knows, and above all his beautiful prayer. They were dressed in black, but about their faces was a radiant whiteness, and when they spoke, they kept their hands hidden in their flowing sleeves. (This a point of Rule with Ursulines as with Carmelites). They distilled into my soul words of ineffable consolation. 'Nish.' I am done."

With this touching allegory in their hearts, the three Ursulines drove off to their appointed field of labor on the Badger and the Two Medicine, hoping and praying that they might realize the Indian's beautiful dream.

In 1892 Mother Amadeus opened two other missions, one at Arlee for Charlos, St. John Berchmans, the other at Pryor for Chief Plenticoos (Many Scalps) St. Charles.

Chief Charlos was one of the noblest of the Flathead race. He loved the Bitter Root valley, the land of his

Fathers, and he refused to leave. But he was betrayed by the sub-chief Arlee, and his signature was falsified and appended to the document sanctioning the transfer of the Flathead tribe to the Jocko. Embittered by this act of duplicity, he refused to follow his people, but remained with a few faithful friends at Old St. Mary's. It was Charlos who refused the hand of Chief Joseph of the Pend d'Oreilles because, he said, "the white man's blood is upon it." But at length, after the death of Arlee, for the sake of the little ones, he consented, but only on condition that he should have a school of his own.

And so, Mother Amadeus, at the cost of a great sacrifice, sent her nuns to the great old man, and whilst he lived they kept school at Arlee. For similar reasons did she open the second Crow Mission at Pryor Creek. That year, too, we took possession of our beautiful new building at St. Peter's. Mother Amadeus was absent, detained by missionary business at Holy Family Mission, but Bishop Brondel himself came up from Helena to preside at the transfer, and he profited by the circumstance of her absence to let his great heart overflow in praise of her wonderful achievements and character.

In 1895 occurred the dreadful A. P. A. movement, and the Government announced that on July, 1896, it would cut off all appropriation. This cruel move left Mother Amadeus penniless and with one thousand Indian girls to support. The move would have killed our Missions if it had killed, too, Mother's ineffable trust in Divine Providence. "A stout heart to a stae brae," and Mother Katherine Drexel and other noble benefactors came to Mother Amadeus' relief.

Thus she kept up our Missions every one of them, not without grinding poverty and anxiety, yet the work for the salvation of souls and the education of the Indian went on. The Rev. Jesuit Fathers withdrew from St. Peter's, but God sent Father Aarts, and in 1898 Mother Amadeus opened a school for white children at Anaconda at the request of another great friend of the Ursulines, the Rev. A. R. Coopman, and by the order of Bishop Brondel.

CHAPTER XV

ROME

In 1900 circulars came from Leo XIII. inviting all the Ursulines to meet in Rome to elect for themselves a Superior General, uniting under one head there, and recasting their venerable constitutions to suit the greater exigencies of modern times.

We had been living this life of greater detachment in the Missions from the beginning. Bishop Gilmour had so ordered when he sent Mother Amadeus and the Ursulines from Toledo to Montana in 1884. Bishop Brondel had sanctioned this arrangement, and upon his first visit *"ad limina"* he had obtained also the sanction of the "Sacred Congregation of the Propaganda," and for Mother Amadeus the title of Superior General of the Ursulines of Montana. He had drawn up the following rules:

Helena, Montana Territory, September 24, 1890.
Circular Letter to Our Beloved Nuns of the Montana Mission.

Beloved Sisters: It is not yet seven years since the first Ursulines for the Indian Missions in Montana came, six in number, under the guidance of Mother Amadeus of Toledo in the Diocese of Cleveland, with the blessing of Rt. Rev. Richard Gilmour, Bishop of Cleveland. They arrived at Miles city, Montana, on the Feast of St. Anthony, January 17, 1884. The same year saw them established at the Sacret Heart Convent of Miles, at St Labré's Mission on Tongue River, amid the Cheyennes, and at St. Peter's Mission for the Blackfeet, where the Novitiate of the Holy Family was founded.

123

Since then, St. Francis Mission, among the Crows; St. Paul's Mission, among the Assiniboines; the Kindergarten among the Flathead at St. Ignatius; and the Holy Family School among the Blackfeet, have opened with such blessings from Heaven that at this moment about seven hundred children receive Christian education, together with board and clothing.

Providence sent noble souls to assist in the work from Ursuline Convents in New York, Philadelphia, Cincinnati, St. Louis, and from different convents in the diocese of Cleveland, so that today the community numbers forty-two members. It has been our great joy to see all work together in harmony and to witness the wonderful result of union.

To preserve and foster this union, we have framed some articles to be incorporated in your rules; we have submitted them to the consideration of all the nuns to elicit their observations, and it rejoiced us greatly to see the unanimity with which they have received them. We now publish these articles putting on them the seal of our authority.

I.

The Mother Superior General is to be elected every six years by one-half of the choir Nuns, *i. e.*, by those who are the oldest in religion. Two-thirds of the votes of the electors are necessary for a valid election, as well as the approval of the Bishop of Helena. Should the Bishop refuse the approval, the electors shall vote again. If a second time the Bishop refuse the approval, then it will be his duty to nominate three nuns, and the electors shall elect one of these three and this one the Bishop cannot but approve. Nuns who are electors, if absent, must send their secret vote to the assembly at the Mother House. The Mother can be re-elected but once in succession.

II.

Mother General's office is to change or appoint special Superiors, to sign documents concerning property. But before doing any of the above acts, she must hear her assistants and consultors. She should have one assistant and two or three consultors, and then to decide what she thinks to be the best before God. Having decided, she must have the approval of the Bishop before accepting, appointing or executing as above.

III.

The Mother House must absolutely belong to the community of the Montana Ursuline Nuns, and to no one else. As to the Mission houses, it depends on circumstances, and the arrangement the Bishop will make with her and the nuns.

IV.

Enclosure is to be enforced according to the rules in the Mother House, and so also in the Mission Houses where they have a community of at least fifteen Sisters.

V.

No Sister, whether cloistered or not, may travel unless she have another Sister with her, or should necessity require it, some other prudent companion. Under these rules Mother Amadeus remains Mother General. The first election of Mother General after six years.

Signed at Helena, on the Feast of St. Theresa, October 15th, 1890.

J. B. BRONDEL, Bishop of Helena.

So we in Montana were living the new life, with ecclesiastical approbation, and we did not need the Union, but the Pope's least wish or word was law to Mother Amadeus of the Heart of Jesus.

For many years, indeed as far back as the Venerable Mary of the Incarnation, the Ursulines had desired to be united in general government. It seemed to be the longing of many of the noblest among them, a thread of gold trailing through the web of their annals from their very first pages, where we find St. Angela called the General of the nascent Order.   Scarcely a distinguished woman in the ranks, though revering the Rule as it stood, but longed for a central and more compact organization.   All felt the need of a greater uniformity and strength to face the growing evils of the day, the greater difficulties.   The methods, and modes of modern education made the change so necessary, that there was scarcely a house of Ursulines, at least in the missionary countries, that had not branched out in imitation of modern teaching communities, and bound to itself some suffragan house or houses.   They were constrained to this change by the force of circumstances, and they relied on the word of the dying Saint that though changes would come, the Order would not perish.   They knew full well that the education of young girls was the pivotal point of the Ursuline life, and they read in their Rule that the Bishop was the Chief Superior.

And yet, in spite of all this, consciences were uneasy, because of the Bulls of Paul V. commanding enclosure and autonomy, and many difficulties arose in daily life which Superiors must settle, and often did settle, contrary to Rule, the dear old insufficient Rule, and, though all felt the discrepancy between the letter of the law and its daily practice, there was no appeal, no bond between the sufferers save that of charity and uniformity of spirit.

Prosperous houses, too, longed to shield and shelter and uplift the weaker ones, yet their word might not have force of law, and they themselves often needed protection when their spirit, their interior life, their spiritual existence was threatened.

And so when Cardinal Serafino Vannutelli's letter came in 1889, just before the opening of our Anaconda house, Mother Amadeus assembled us in Chapter, and never did she seem grander, more like an Ursuline. She told us that the Pope's wish was law for a religious, that it was an honor to have been noticed by so august a person as Leo XIII., and that, therefore, we had but one thing to do: obey. Her face, her words, her voice, made a deep impression on us, so that even they who had not lived our life long enough to know that Union was necessary, felt that though open in form, the question was closed in fact by the Pope's word. To each one of our houses Mother Amadeus sent a copy of the Bishop's letter to her, requiring the local Superior to assemble the nuns in her house, to have each write to the Bishop sending him her sealed and secret vote. This was done immediately and exactly. This is what the Bishop wrote to Mother Amadeus and what she sent to each house, together with her own translation of Mother Julian's letter explaining Pope Leo's desires in the matter of union:

Helena, Montana, August 25, 1899.
Rev. Mother Mary Amadeus, Superior General, St. Peter, Montana:

Rev. Mother: I have received a circular letter dated Rome, 21st July, 1899, and signed by S. Cardinal Vannutelli, Prefect of the Sacred Congregation of Bishops and Regulars. The Cardinal says: that among the religious institutes to which, by apostolic approbation and under the watchfulness of prelates, was entrusted the noble work of training in piety and science the young ladies, the Order of Consecrated Virgins which has its name from St. Ursula is eminent by its antiquity not less than by virtue and merits.

But as the Monasteries of Ursulines, though united by

charity are not held together by a bond of true association, it happens, not rarely that some of their colleges cannot easily obtain the end they have in view, because they have not enough of the necessary means, nor the hope to obtain them from the other families of the same Order, because they are separated. To obviate these incommodities and difficulties, this Sacred Congregation of Bishops and Regulars, last year thought proper to receive with benevolence the postulations of some bishops tending toward a union between the colleges of Ursulines, and therefore, by decree of October, 1898, decided that, whenever some of the families of Ursuline Nuns, existing in different parts of the Catholic world, asked to unite in particular congregations, their prayers and wishes should be granted most willingly. Lately, from some Ursuline families, existing in different regions, letters have been sent to obtain that the whole Order should be united into one body, according to the institutes, which born in this century, were approved by the Holy See.

Undoubtedly, the Holy See is not used to easily change what has been rightly constituted and made firm by a long course of time, unless the changes which are asked for seem to suit better the changed times and lead to obtain the purpose of the institute better and more efficaciously. Therefore, the Congregation, before it constitutes anything in that matter, judges most opportune to know what the Bishops and nuns themselves think about it. Therefore the Bishop is asked to consider this matter with attention and diligence, and to express his opinion to the Sacred Congregation, after having inquired what the religious think of it.

But as it is important that the religious make known with full liberty what they think about it, it is proper that within the proper time indicated to them, during which they may weigh the matter before God, each one opens her mind by suffrage altogether secret.

But the Sisters should understand: First: That this union means only this: that these things be constituted by common counsel which seem proper and necessary for the ruling of the whole institute, preserving as much as possible the laws, constitution and customs by which every monastery is legitimately governed.

Second: They should know also that the form of union would be so constituted that First, the General Superioress, elected for a certain time by the delegates of each monastery should reside in Rome, together with the general council, likewise elected by the same delegates. Second: That the whole Order be divided into divers provinces, presided over by a Provincial Superior with her council. Third: Everywhere the formula of religious profession will be the same, embracing the three vows of obedience, of poverty, and of chastity, no mention being made of the fourth vow of educating young girls. For in the vow of obedience, made according to the form of the Constitutions of the Order, this vow is evidently contained.

These matters were ordered brought to the knowledge of the bishops by command of our Most Holy Lord, Leo XIII. Therefore, Rev. Mother Mary Amadeus, please bring to the knowledge of the professed Ursulines of Montana, this matter, and after collecting the secret votes of all, please send them to us, that we may correspond to the desires of His Eminence, the Cardinal Prefect of the Sacred Congregation of the Bishops and Regulars.

Yours with blessing,

JOHN B. BRONDEL, *Bishop of Helena.*

When the Ursulines of Montana were called upon to send their secret votes to the Bishop of Helena on the subject of union, the votes were favorable to general government. Mother Amadeus of the Heart of Jesus was therefore summoned to attend the General Chapter in Rome. She started on October 25, 1890, with her Ursuline companion and a little Flathead girl. The journey was a long one. Mother Amadeus said one day to her companions: "We three are starting out alone into the unknown. We have no guide but the star of our obedience to Leo XIII. The three kings going to

the crib are our models and protectors. I have not
heard of any other Ursulines heeding this summons,
but even if I were sure that I were the only one to heed
it, still I should go on to Rome." So these three wise
ones from the western wilds traveled eastward following the star.

In New York they were joined by a dear benefac-
tress, Miss L———, who went with them to Rome, paying their way. She, too, was obeying Leo XIII., who
had called all who were free to do so to go to Rome
to gain the indulgences of the Holy Year.

On November 1, 1900, the *Aquitaine* set sail. Mother
Amadeus remained at the stern watching the revered
form of her great friend, the Very Rev. James Kent
Stone, C. P., who stood there, blessing the ship sailing so gallantly forth into the unknown. She never
wavered. She never changed, firmly, supernaturally she
obeyed. She had done great things for God. She stood
in the high light of her success, respected by priests
and bishops, beloved beyond human reckoning by the
nuns, revered by all the Indian tribes of Montana. What
could she wish more? There was one thing. The saints
have strange longings. She desired humilitations and
keener suffering.

She feared she was having her reward in this world
and that there would be nothing left for the next. So
Mother Amadeus prayed amid the sunlit waters of the
Atlantic on that serene All Saints Day for those minor
chords that make the harmony of love. And quickly
did the Divine Lover answer that sublime prayer, as
one who stands and waits with the royal gift in His
hands.

In Paris the missionaries were entertained by the

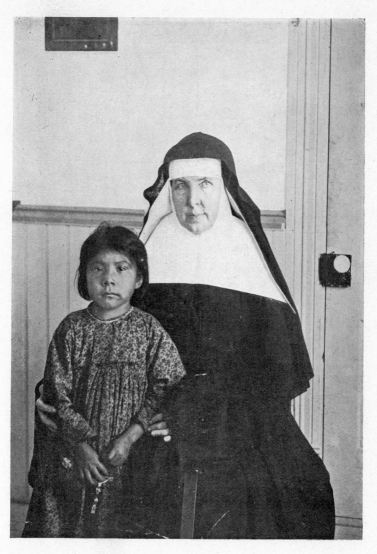

MOTHER AND ANGELA PRETTY EAGLE.

Ladies of the Sacred Heart at the far-famed Rue de Varennes. Mother Digby, the Superior General, was so much touched by the generous obedience of the Ursuline missionaries, so much interested in the project of union, occurring as it did on the first centenary of their foundation, that she received them with most gracious, generous hospitality. She looked long at Mother Amadeus with those penetrating eyes of hers, and read there the wonderful secret of sanctity. So unconscious of merit was she, so unassuming, and yet so full of courage and determination. God makes wonderful and beautiful things.

Still Mother Amadeus had no tidings of other Ursuline travelers to Rome, nor could she tell her generous hostess anything about the coming Chapter. On Sunday night, November 11th, they boarded the train for Rome. As they entered the train, her companion said: "Mother, I think there are some nuns in the next coach. Perhaps they are Ursulines." "Go and see," she answered. "Are You Ursulines?" inquired Sister, her head in the next compartment, for there were six in number and wearing different costumes. "Yes," came the answer. "Are you going to Rome?" "Yes." Then the first comers became questioners in their turn. "Are you Ursulines?" "Yes." Are you going to Rome?" Yes," and the six made room for two more, and the eight Ursulines spent the night talking about Rome and union. Two of these nuns were from Holland, two from the Rocky Mountains, and the rest from various French communities, and though they had never met, and though they wore different dresses, still all were most closely united in heart and spirit. Mother Amadeus made a deep impression on these and all the members of the Chapter. Their hearts were lifted up to see their sisters from the Missions coming so great a distance to link hands with them in the all-important movement.

Mother Amadeus and Mother St. Julian of Blois both had the title of Superior General, and both headed the ranks in the Chapter hall. Whenever Mother Amadeus rose to speak, which she did in French, the language of the assembly, Monsignor Battandier, Protonotary Apostolic, and the Very Rev. Joseph Lemius, Procurator General of the Oblates of Mary Immaculate, President and Vice-president of the gathering, listened with marked attention and respect. In Mother Amadeus the Order saw exemplified and accomplished the form it wished to assume, and she became a centre, not only for America and the Congregation of Paris, but for all. It is my firm belief, and others have since confirmed my opinion, that Mother Amadeus of the Heart of Jesus would have been elected to the first position in the giving of the Chapter, had not the electors feared that they would thereby cripple the work of the Missions, so dear to all those apostolic hearts. Whenever she entered the chapter hall, all eyes turned toward her. Mother Ignatius of Frankfort, who was elected Vicar, was quick to detect the firmness hidden beneath that most winning maternal smile. "Mother Amadeus is gentle—yes," she remarked, "but I see great firmness too, in the corners of her mouth."

Mother Amadeus' piety and fervor in Rome were very remarkable. At every step she gave evidence of the deep spirit of faith so eminently hers. The day that the union was voted, she was confined to bed. The two vote-takers were conducted to her cell. It was

November 14, 1900. Her face bore an expression of sublime purity and strength as she wrote with a smile that smile which means the love of Our Lord alone, a name that signed away her title of Superior General and placed her in the rank and file. I knelt beside her. My heart stood still, though I was accustomed to look upon her heroism and forgetfulness of self. But when we reached the chapter hall, and Mother's eight votes for union were counted—she represented each one of our Mission houses —a suppressed murmur of wonder and admiration broke from the assembly and Father Lemius said aloud: *"C'est beau cela*—that is splendid."

Indeed, Mother Amadeus' vote for union was one worth having. She presented the little Indian lassie to the great Pope, and he blessed her and all our dear benefactors, and accepted for the Museum of the Vatican an Indian dress and war bonnet.

Mother Amadeus' artistic soul reveled in the splendors of St. Peter's. She was absolutely lost in prayer at the tomb of the Apostles. She seemed to be lifted up when the Pope was carried in above our heads in the *"Sedia Gestatoria,"* when our little darling was lifted one day in the arms of the stalwart Swiss guard up to the level of the Pope's eyes as he passed giving his blessing, and he asked, "Who is this starry-eyed child clad in buckskin?" The child said to Mother Amadeus when she was set down beside her: "Mother, I thought I was in Heaven."

Cardinals and prelates were frequent visitors to our assembly, and all, before leaving the house, desired to speak with the Mother from the Rocky Mountains and to listen to the little lassie of the Flathead tribe sing, accompanying herself on the mandolin. Cardinals Guistini, Gotti, Satolli, Macchi, Logue, were henceforth Mother Amadeus' friends as were our own dear Cardinals Gibbons, Farley and O'Connell.

When our "Little Child of God" died on her return to St. Peter's Mission, Mother Amadeus sent word to the Pope, and he himself spoke her panegyric: "I remember her well, the blessed little child."

Mother St. Julian was elected first Superior General of the canonically united Ursulines. At dinner that day the new Superior General was congratulated by the nuns in eleven different languages, and eleven is a mystic number among the Ursulines: In French, Italian, Spanish, English, German, Latin, Javanese, Gaelic, Portuguese, Dutch and Indian. This latter toast fell to our Mother, and she spoke in the tongue of the war-like Cheyennes to the great delight of all. These simple greetings were a rare proof of the catholicity of the prolific Order, during the many years of its vicissitudes. All suns had seen it.

Mother Amadeus was confirmed in her charge of the Montana Missions with the added title of "Visitor with the powers of Provincial." Her first care was to wait upon the newly elected Superior General and obtain permission to open Missions in Alaska. Mother St. Julian, too, was a great-hearted woman. She enthusiastically granted the permission, begging Mother Amadeus to go to Alaska herself to see that the Missions were put on a proper footing. How gladly she would go, also, said this apostolic woman. She then invited our Mother to go with her for a few days rest to the old far-famed monastery of Calvi.

The rugged fortress convent of "Calvi dell' Umbria" runs up and down the hill in stone walls six feet thick.

Much picturesque beauty, but little comfort is there.
One hundred and fifty years before, it had been the
dwelling of the last Marquis Ferrini, who, dying, left it
to the Bishop of Narni with the proviso that a convent
be founded in his ancestral manor. Failing this, in one
hundred years, the majestic pile was to be given to the
poor of the surrounding country as their heritage. The
last Marquis Ferrini died, and time stole on as it will
steal on in the *"dolce far niente"* atmosphere of lovely
Italy. One morning, 364th of the 99th year, a beggar who
was wont to ply his trade at the portal of the still ten-
antless Ferrini mansion, said carelessly to a passerby:
"Tomorrow, I shall be rich." Swiftly flew his words
to the Bishop, and a rider, booted and spurred, was off
to the neighboring monastery, and that night three
Benedictine nuns slept in the eyrie. They had come
only to hold the fort. In a short time they were re-
placed by six holy Ursulines from Rome. I call them
holy, for in the memorable year of the union, their
bodies still stood erect against the walls of the monastery vault, awaiting the resurrection.

Many and touching were the memories clinging to
the old Calvi convent as Mother Amadeus wonderingly
beheld it. So famous did it become in the annals of the
country that it was not called the Monastery of Calvi,
but the mountain town itself rather was called "Calvi
of the Monastery." In 1870, the year of the great Italian spoliation, the government undertook to confiscate
our house, to transform it into a mountain fortress, but
the peasants rose to a man and said: "Hands off, this
is our property." And so were the sacred walls saved,
but iniquitous laws forbade the reception of subjects
until at last three only were left in the community.

Mother Crocefissa, the only professed nun, faithfully rang the big monastery bell three times a day for office, and then went alone into the chapel to chant it. Mother Jacinta was for thirty years a postulant waiting to take the habit, zealously teaching the district school to support her sisters. One friend they had, Monsignor Bonvecchi, Vicar General of the diocese, who came regularly over from Narni to hear their confessions. One day, seeing their hopeless condition, he proposed that they should cede the property to the Benedictines of the neighborhood and they themselves become Benedictines. "What," exclaimed the still undaunted Madre Crocefiissa, "an Ursuline become a Benedictine? Let the Benedictines rather come over and become Ursulines." Her sublime fidelity, her strong faith, were rewarded. Mother St. Julian and the community of Blois took pity on their misery as well as on that of the even less fortunate Roman house, a large-hearted charity that merited for them prosperity, and for the whole Order the blessing of union. For the lesser union "Blois-Rome-Calvi" became the nucleus of the greater ones.

When Mother Amadeus visited Calvi one sunny day in early December, 1900, she drove in an uncovered buggy, with her two companions from the railroad station, Civita Castellana, over the hills through Magliano to the little town perched so high up on the mountain side, that she wondered how the patient builders ever lifted there the stone for their building, and how the mules climbed up to deliver the daily provisions from below. But most of the lesser Italian cities are close to the sky, and Calvi boasts great age. They say that the hoof-beats of SS. Sebastian and Pancratius echoed on the flagging; the great town portal, they

know, is the work of Julius Cæsar. The peasants had
to put their shoulders to the carriage wheels to push
us up the last acclivity. That night we heard the monastery bell tolling all night—it was December 9th—to
commemorate the passage of the Angels over Calvi
carrying the Holy House to Loreto.

It is a blessed land of blessed memories!

CHAPTER XVI

Homeward

FROM Calvi, Mother Amadeus' way led through Assisi, Loreto, Florence, Milan, Genoa, Lyons, Paray-le-Monial, Paris, Boulogne, Havre, Cherbourg. The night of Janury 1st, her party assisted at Midnight Mass in the great Basilica and in the Holy House of Loreto. The monster church was over-crowded when they entered with the first strains of the Pontifical High Mass. So great was the crowd that, inch by inch, patiently threading their way, they reached the communion railing just at the *"Domine non sum dignus."* One of the attendant priests, noticing Mother Amadeus as all did wherever she passed, made a sign for her to enter the sanctuary. He placed her at the foot of the altar where, she, first of all that expectant multitude, and her little Indian girl second, received Our Lord on that last night of the Holy Year.

Our Lord in so many little ways of ineffable delicacy, strove to console Mother Amadeus. At Naples, she assisted once at the liquefaction of the blood of St. Januarius, and so great were the faith and the fervor with which she venerated the holy relic, that, when he had passed the crystal tube to all, the officiating priest, unasked, brought it to Mother Amadeus who received it with the look of a surprised and delighted child. He suffered her to keep it twenty minutes in her arms, the martyr blood bubbling up against the blood of the virgin heart. Was this grace given to prepare her for martyrdom?

138

Mother Amadeus went to Assisi as a pilgrim in the third-class coach, but an amusing experience to our little girl, who fortunately did not understand a word of Italian, dissuaded her from a second trial of this act of penance. We were crowded in the poor coach with many soldiers who had also been paying their devotions to the beloved *"Poverello di Christe."* One of these, having no doubt forgotten all the good resolutions formed at the tomb of St. Francis, was lost in admiration before the little Flathead girl. He at once spontaneously offered himself to the unconscious child of nine years, who never knew or suspected what he was saying, Mother answering for her, that the child was altogether too young. In Rome the porter of the "Collegio Romano" had said on looking at the little one: *"Figlia mia, il sole none e piu bello di te*—My daughter, the sun alone outshines thy beauty." Mother Amadeus' heart leaped with joy to hear this praise of the saintly old religious to her little unconscious Indian maiden.

In Milan Mother Amadeus had again to defend the child, for Countess N——— wished to adopt her and to make her the sole heiress of a large estate. Nor was a first refusal sufficient. The lady, childless and lonely, in her splendor, brought to bear many powerful influences to bend Mother Amadeus' will in this matter. In Florence, in Paris where the travelers reveled in all the exquisite treasures of art, the child delighted Mother by her attention, her appreciation. Fearing she might see what she should not, Mother Amadeus had instructed her companion to lead the little one away from any objectionable picture or statue, but this precaution proved unnecessary. The child always stopped before the pictures her own little heart understood and loved, those of Jesus, Mary and Joseph. At Paray-le-Monial, Mother prayed long, long before the sacred shrine and at the tomb of Father de la Colombière. What passed there, it is not given to human tongue to tell. But she rose from her prayer greatly comforted and strengthened, with that air, tender and commanding, which silenced all inquiry.

One of the great talents of Mother Amadeus of the Heart of Jesus was her talent for writing. Indeed, her letters have been compared by our best critics to the letters of the great St. Theresa. Her command of the king's English spoke the tenderness and strength of her heart. By her pen she was enabled to build up and support God's work. Never wearying, always delighting her benefactors, she reached their inmost generous selves. Would that space were granted us to quote freely from her wonderful correspondence! We could quote of her the words of Father Faber: "On days of joy and moments of triumphant festivity, then it is that the skillful Fathers (and Mothers—parenthesis is ours) know how to lay sweet siege to the hearts of men, and with gentle craft, to win their wealth from them for the little ones of Christ, and none are givers so generous as those who are distinguished by an especial devotion to the Blessed Sacrament."

No less touching were the letters she wrote to her nuns:

February, 21, 1901.

Aboard the *Kaiser Wilhelm:*

What a sad parting. Never shall I forget it. Your little bark moving one way, and mine another. You are constantly in my mind. My poor little girl has been sick all

day. She can retain nothing on her stomach. I am obliged
to stay with her all day in the cabin. She is indeed a poor
sailor. I do not feel so well as on the *Aquitaine*. Every
thing is very grand. The people, too, are very kind. Good-
bye for a little while. Would this were the last instead of
the first of six times three hundred and sixty-five days.

2-25-01. We are having a most disastrous trip. Everyone on board with the exception of a few gentlemen has
succumbed. I am making a strong fight to keep up, but it
is only a feint. I am so sick that I do not know myself.
My companion has been sick from the first hour up to the
present moment. She can retain nothing. Ditto for myself. We expect to land tomorrow afternoon.

2-26. The waves are furious. They toss this mam-
moth ship as though it were a toy. Such rolling and tossing
I never knew before. We are pitched in every direction.
No one can sleep at night on account of storms. We have
no thunder and lightning, but only wind and such waves.
This morning one of the sailors was nearly washed over-
board whilst washing the deck. I have just returned from
a visit to the third-class passengers. Such a time as I had
to keep up. I was afraid the purser would notice it. I
begged to go to the hospital, but he put me off till tomorrow,
saying it was too rough for any lady to be on her feet. I
am afraid some little babies may die without baptism. I
fear there must be some sickness on board, for I see the
doctor does not want me to go to the hospital. I shall try
again tomorrow. Poor Little One and I, we look at each
other in mute sympathy, too sick to speak a word. I am
sitting propped up, writing on the washstand. She lying
down covered up, yellow as an orange. She is bitterly sick.
Yesterday it took me three hours to comb out her hair. It
was in a perfect mat. No comb could go through it. She
had been so hurried for the last three days before we started
that she neglected to comb it. That is why she looked so
frowsy. I made believe I was going to cut it off if she did
not stand the process of my combing out its snarls. So my
little lady submitted to the operation very cheerfully rather
than lose her shining locks.

Good-bye, my own dear one. Be faithful to God, your friends and your country.

Your own,
SISTER MARY AMADEUS.

Again she writes:

We arrived at 10 P. M. February 26, and landed at 10 A. M. February 27.

Every one is excited over the union. Now is the time to do some good. I am working hard. Keep up good spirits whatever we do. Let us do it earnestly. You know I'll do nothing by halves. Principle! Principle! I am suffering a martyrdom for want of money.* * *

Thus we see that Mother Amadeus' home journey was a sad one. Reaching New York she threaded her way back to Montana, visiting the great Convent of the "Pines" at Chatham and all the other Ursuline Convents within reach, speaking in favor of union, encouraging the doubtful and giving to all news of Rome and the great Roman Union.

CHAPTER XVII

MOTHER AMADEUS CRIPPLED FOR LIFE

In Montana the cross awaited Mother Amadeus of the Heart of Jesus, the cross she had asked of the Crucified Spouse. "Many pages of this story," says little Thérèse of Lisieux, "will never be read on earth. There are sufferings that are never to be disclosed here below. Our Lord has jealously reserved to Himself the right to reveal their merit and glory in the dear vision when all veils shall be removed."

Mother Amadeus peacefully continued her ministrations. Indeed on October 2d, she left St. Peter's with four companions to re-open the new and beautiful convent she had erected at Miles City. The nuns noticed that, contrary to her wont, Mother Amadeus seemed to dread this journey. Day after day, she put it off, and when finally she started, she led the nuns to the chapel, and here, after praying her arms extended in the form of a cross, she walked slowly to the outer portal, and, turning, bade them good-bye and recommended in seraphic tones, charity, union, prayerfulness. She who had always walked away with so much buoyancy, returned after she had descended a few steps, and again in words of fire, recommended union, charity, prayerfulness. Her four companions, the weeping nuns, marveled greatly.

At Helena, the five boarded the Northern Pacific train which on the morning of October 4, 1902, had brought them safe to a station near Billings called

143

Rapid Sidings. Here they were startled by a deadly crash. The westbound Burlington train, running at full speed, crashed into the eastbound Northern Pacific. The engines telescoped and took fire. Three train hands were killed, and many passengers were injured. The nuns were safe, but, self-forgetting Mother Amadeus, walked hastily forward that she might minister consolation and comfort to the wounded and the dying. As she did so, a car was rudely coupled to hers, the two suddenly backed up that they might escape burning and she was rudely thrown back on to the edge of her seat. A head-on collision. A cry of agony, only one, and she lay helpless on the floor, unable to move. The nuns hastened to her side, but the slightest movement caused her intense pain. Their train was hanging over the verge of a sharp declivity. But at length, a car was backed up, and Mother Amadeus in the agony of crucifixion, was lifted on a stretcher, through the car window, over the embankment into the caboose that brought her at last to Billings hospital.

One of the brave Montana men who tenderly lifted Mother Amadeus in the hour of her great pain was James William Wimsett. Himself a non-Catholic, he had married a Catholic wife and to make a home for her and the children just then was working at Rapid Sidings. After fearlessly rebuking the "boss"—for the fatal accident was due to rash and daring disobedience to orders—he set about helping. He was struck by Mother Amadeus' wonderful smile, her brave cheerfulness. "If I am ever injured," he said afterward to his wife, "I hope I may act as Mother Amadeus did." And in 1914 he was injured on that very spot and carried, as she had been, to Billings' hospital. The memory of the saintly face he had beheld in 1902 cheered and strengthened him, and guided him safe, before he died, into the arms of the Church that is the Mother of such heroisms.

Even in this hour of extreme need Mother Amadeus never forgot her duty as Superior. Taking with her two of her companions, she appointed the other two to continue their journey to Miles City and there, with two boarders they had brought with them, and with another Ursuline who had just come down from the Crow Mission, to open school on the appointed day. But whilst all this was transpiring, precious time was lost, and the first help available proved unskilled and insufficient. The nuns begged Mother Amadeus to return at once to Helena to her friend, the eminent surgeon, Dr. Treacy. But she answered: "The poor cannot afford those comforts. Where God willed that they should fall, there does He also will them to be cared for."

One of the nuns who had witnessed the accident tells of it a few hours afterwards in the following terms:

On train Park City, 3:30 P. M. October 4, 1902.
Dear ———— and all our Dear Sisters:

Perhaps you have heard of the dreadful wreck. You must be very anxious, and though I feel my letter will be a very poor one, for my mind and heart and body are very tired, I think it may be a relief to you to know the truth, sad as it is.

On October 3d we left with Mother for Miles City. At 5 o'clock our train and the westbound train collided. The engines exploded and a number of cars were burned. Mother was hurt, how badly we do not yet know. She is now in Billings hospital and Sr. C—is with her. After the collision Mother was just starting to walk down the car to see what she could do for the wounded. Two men were killed, one burned alive, the other smashed to pieces. Suddenly another car was joined violently to Mother's. Not expecting the shock, she was thrown from her feet, but fell heavily on her right hip and could not rise. She has not been able to move a quarter of an inch since without pain so excruciating, as causes her to cry out. Six doctors came to the rescue, some from Livingston, some from Billings. They were most attentive to Mother. She was lifted from the car on a stretcher, men passing her on this out of the window over a steep bank. It was a most painful, risky undertaking, but Mother's pain was so great that she could not be taken out any other way. The men were grand. I do not know how they ever got her out. At about 9 o'clock an engine from Billings came up to us and took the wounded on to the hospital. Mother went on a stretcher in the caboose car. It was too hard to try to get her into the Pullman, as the slightest move caused her anguish.

Generous, unselfish Mother Amadeus herself wrote a few hours after she has been lifted into bed.

My Own Dear Child:

Just imagine me laid up a cripple, sent home today for the crutches you laid down. I am so sorry to hear you are ill. Please write me all about yourself. Mother General wrote me a very kind letter which I shall try to answer as soon as I am able. Pray that I may get a pass on the railroad and some free freight in compensation for my injury. I am praying constantly for you, and offering my sufferings for each member of your dear family. Please pray and ask prayers for my speedy recovery, for I have much to do before winter sets in.   Your own,

SISTER MARY AMADEUS.

The cane Mother Amadeus took up was never dropped. It was a constant cross, but she never uttered a word of complaint. She kept repeating in deep recollection the words: "May the most high, the most holy, the most just will of God be done! May it be ever

HOMES OF ESKIMO CLIFF DWELLERS, KING ISLAND, ALASKA.

praised and glorified." And when the crisis was over, she would turn to her nuns and smile. Her unselfishness, her cheerful acquiescence to God's will it is not in my power to describe. It lasted, sunny and unbroken, from October 4, 1902, until November 10, 1919, when she saw face to face Him Who permitted her affliction. Nor did it ever arrest her ministrations to her dear Missions.

The nuns in their distress had recourse first to God and then to Bishop Brondel, who immediately sent Mother Amadeus the following dispatch: "Come at once to Dr. Treacy in Helena." And she, in obedience, was lifted again, and in St. John's Hospital, Helena, received all the care the most distinguished physician, the most careful nursing could give. All Helena crowded to her bedside. Notable among the many, were Mrs. J. K. Toole, wife of the Governor of Montana, and her sister, Miss Rosecrans, daughters of our great general; Mrs. Col Saunders, the Misses Fortune, Mrs. C. Power, Mrs. Major Maginnis, Mrs. Senator Carter; names that shine like golden lights on Montana's record. Mrs. Maginnis said of Mother Amadeus during those days of anguish: "She is a woman of immense sweetness." She lay immobilized for nine weeks, with heavy weights suspended from her feet, and a smile, a word of counsel and consolation for every one. At her side sat every day, her great, first friend in the Mission life, the Rt. Rev. J. B. Brondel, first Bishop of Helena. Upon one thing the Bishop insisted, that Mother Amadeus should heed Dr. Treacy's order to go to California for her convalescence, that her heart might recover, at the sea level, from the fearful shock it had sustained. At the Bishop's request, Mother General

in Rome sent a cable saying that as soon as she was
able to travel, Mother Amadeus was to be taken to
Corodano Beach. And Dr. Treacy himself gently lifted
her into the cab, and from the cab into the sleeper as
soon as she was able to make use of crutches and wheel-
ing chair. With two companions she started for the
coast, past the sublime scenes of Mt. Shasta and together they beheld for the first time the majestic Pacific Ocean.

"All for the Sacred Heart," she writes on April 3,
1903. We left Helena for California via Portland.
Mesdames Martin, Finn and Perry, Mamie and Lucy
Flinn, came to the station to see us off. Dr. Treacy
carried me from the carraige into the car with ad-
mirable skill and strength. We arrived at Portland at
9:45 P. M. and went to St. Vincent's hospital. Palm
Sunday I went to Sunday Mass for the first time in six
months. *Deo Gratias et Mariæ!* Branches of blessed
palm were passed around during the reading of the
Passion, whilst the sisters sang softly in minor keys
and a Monsignor read the gospel.

"About 4 P. M. we saw the great Mt. Shasta. At
Shasta Springs we drank of the water, soda, iron and
sulphur, very fine and sparkling. About 8 A. M. we
arrived at Oakland and took the San Joaquin inside
track. . . . . We passed today the celebrated San
Juan Capistrano Mission and had a good view of it."

Mother Amadeus was deeply impressed by her first
view of the Pacific. The waves that caressed Coronado
Beach, kissed also in their outward journey, the rough
and the rugged shores of Alaska, the beloved. The
thought that, as soon as she recovered, she and her
nuns would go to Alaska to minister there, was ever

uppermost in her mind as they wheeled her back and forth upon the glorious beach or drove her down past the Mexican line to Tia Juana to be the guest of Mrs. Stephens. This lady, a convert, was a pupil of the Sacred Heart Convent of Manhattanville; her husband, Anson P. Stephens was a Harvard classmate of Mother Amadeus' friend, the Passionist Superior Provincial, writer, organizer, the Very Rev. James Kent Stone, better known as Father Fidelis. Every morning Mother Amadeus would send her companions off to Mass in the church. Locking her in alone in the little convent cottage, they went with anxious hearts, and returned as quickly as they could along the avenues of blooming pepper trees, to prepare her room for the coming of Our Lord. Her heart was steeped in the love of the Most Blessed Sacrament. This the kind pastor knew, and he would follow the returning nuns bearing his ineffable Burden.

Before Mother Amadeus had recovered, however, she was called to St. Paul's Mission, Montana, by the illness of one of the nuns. Though not really able, she hastened to comfort her dear sister. Sister recovered, but Mother Amadeus was stricken a second time with pneumonia, and was anointed by the superior, the Rev. Father Vasta, S.J.

But she recovered in due time and went about with her crutches and cane (henceforth her inseparable companions), from Mission to Mission with unabated vigilance ruling and fertilizing the field.

It is at this period of her life that we must chronicle her trips to Rome.

On one of her homeward trips she stopped at the abbey of Monte Cassino. Here letters from His Eminence Cardinal Satolli assured her a true Benedictine welcome. Another Benedict and Scholastica ruled here —the mitred Lord Abbot Krug, the abbey, his sister, St. Scholastica's convent at the foot of the hill. Both were most gracious. The Lord Abbot kept Mother Amadeus three days as his guest, leaving at her disposal the hospice at the foot of the hill. He explained his plans for the restoration of the monastery and basilica. He appointed one of his most learned monks to show her in his stead the history of St. Benedict and the great Order which his artists were writing in mosaic upon the walls. Every morning this holy religious waited at the great monastery portal until Mother Amadeus arrived from the hospice, conducted her to a private oratory where he offered the Most Holy Sacrifice. After Mass and thanksgiving followed breakfast, with true monastic hospitality, and then a visit through the historic pile, its libraries and workshops. What a rest it was for the tired missionary! What a joy to a mind and soul like hers so well prepared to drink it all in!

At Genoa Mother Amadeus stopped with the Sisters of Charity of Nevers, some of whom had been novices with Bernadette, and there awaited the sailing of the *Montevideo* of the Royal Spanish line. Leaving Genoa on June 21st, the ship stopped at Barcelona, Naples, Malaga, Cadiz, to the great delight of the nuns on board. Besides the three Missionary Ursulines, there were two from Spain, five Sisters of Hope, five priests. Mother Amadeus visited the splendid Cathedrals everywhere. Of Malaga she writes, "Malaga is one of the most ancient and also one of the most celebrated Spanish ports on the Mediterranean. The exuberance of vegetation surpasses all that can be imagined. Abound orange and fig groves; sugar cane and cotton grow luxuriantly, melons, almonds, pomegranates, Japanese quince—Malaga's wine is the celebrated Muscat. The Cathedral of the Incarnation is imposing. The arms of Philip II. and Mary the Catholic of England (1544) appear everywhere, and here are those exquisite stalls, the world's most famous wood-carvings."

One Sunday, it was the feast of the Precious Blood, the captain sent word that Mass would be on deck. The sea was unruffled, the boat was splendidly decked with Spanish flags and the picture of "Nuestra Senora del Carmine," patroness of the navy. The crew to a man was in line, Mother Amadeus and her nuns having seats of honor. At the appointed hour, the chaplain appeared accompanied by two sailors in spotless white uniforms, who stood motionless, holding lighted torches whilst the august Sacrifice unfolded. It was very solemn, this Mass upon the deep, whilst the waves caressed the *Montevideo* and the wonder of Transubstantiation was wrought before a reverent gathering.

The passengers were Cuban or Spanish and their conversation was lofty, Catholic and interesting. One of the sailors "Tomaso" had fought in the Spanish-American war, and he told Mother Amadeus how at "Santiago de Cuba" he thanked God that he fell into American, not Cuban hands.

In Rome Mother Amadeus made many new friends, and strengthened the friendships already made. Cardinal Satolli greeted her one day at the door of the Lateran, though he knew her only by her great works, with the question: "Mother Amadeus, have you a heart of gold?" Cardinal Logue, Primate of all Ireland, invited her to breakfast with him at the Irish College on St.

Patrick's Day. She had frequent audiences with Pope Pius X., who used to smile and say: "Mother, you and I both have a *'bastone.'* " He loaded the great foundress with kindness and with privileges. Among her numerous friends were many distinguished religious, and that other great foundress, Mother Cabrini.

Mother Amadeus of the heart of Jesus enjoyed rare privileges. She assisted at the consistory in which her distinguished friend and helper Monsignor Bisleti was raised to the cardinalate. She saw Pius X. consecrate the first fourteen French Bishops after Combes had broken the Concordat, and established the evanescent "Association Culturelles" to take the place of the immortal Catholic Church founded by Christ, the Lord. She beheld the seven altars erected on either side of the Papal altar in the apse of St. Peter's beneath the chair of Peter; she saw the fifteen sacred Hosts lifted at the same moment, the fifteen chalices as if raised by one hand for the redemption of the world. She was one of the 60,000 in the basilica to hear the silver trumpets call out the: *"Tu es Petrus."* Pressed one day to tell what his plan was with regard to the "Associations Culturelles." Pius X. pointed to the Tabernacle of his private oratory and said: "He has not yet told me what to do." The consecration of fourteen bishops, the resignation of the Bishops of Dijon and Laval which he had accomplished with his *"Mano di veluto, braccio di ferro"* was the great, silent Pontiff's magnificent and masterly response.

Before returning to the United States, Mother Amadeus visited, with ineffable consolation, the shrine of Our Lady of Good Counsel at Genezzano, Our Lady of Lourdes, Our Lady of Victory and Montmartre in Paris.

She was to meet Mother General at Havré and go with her to the United States. But the interval, the delicious interval, she spent in the blessed land where her father and mother were born, the "Isle of the Saints," introduced everywhere by letters from Cardinal Logue. The Carmelites and Ursulines throughout the Green Isle received with enthusiasm this daughter of the martyrs, of the kings of Iregan.

Refreshed by all these delightful sights and scenes, she stepped aboard *La Lorraine* to pilot the first Superior General of the Ursulines in her first visitation of the great United States. On this occasion, Mother Amadeus was formally installed first Provincial of the "North of the United States," with her seat at Middletown, N. Y. Here on August 15, 1906, was opened the first general Novitiate of the "Canonically United Ursulines," and the wheels of the new government began to turn with the greatest of all the Ursulines at its head. Mother Amadeus then went with the Mother General to Montana, showing her the beauties of our vast land as it stretches from sea to sea, making her feel the comforts, the facilities of its travel. At St. Peter's both assisted at the election of Mother St. Francis, "the humble violet of the Rockies," as Mother Amadeus' successor in the local government of the Missions.

In New York, without money and a stranger, Mother Amadeus of the Heart of Jesus began the work of organizing the vast first Ursuline Province. Cardinal Farley honored her with his esteem, his friendship, his help, and her magnetism and power did the rest. She succeeded in this most difficult task. Meeting many, she won the hearts of all in this new field, and not one ever heard an uncharitable word fall from her lips. Yet her conversation was varied, animated, sympathetic. She had many bitter trials, she met with many heavy crosses, but she lifted and carried them. She led a life of incessant activity, walking painfully with a cane and counting one sleepless night after another. In 1905, she sent her first missionaries to Alaska, and as soon as she was free to do so, she made ready to fly on the wings of love to that field of labor and privation. This winning, successful, highly cultured Superior was ever a model of austere penance. Such penance fills the heart with the spirit of fortitude and joy.

As a child Mother Amadeus of the Heart of Jesus, loved the sea gulls above all the birds. She used to repeat again and again the little verse: "If thou wert a bird, what bird wouldst thou be? A frolicsome gull on the billowy sea?" From the deck of the *S. S. Victoria* she watched these graceful creatures of the air, spreading their lavender wings, circling about and resting lovingly at last on the rugged, desolate shores of Northern Alaska, making it beautiful and peopling it with memories. To us they seem a picture of the soaring and lofty soul of Mother Amadeus of the Heart of Jesus.

CHAPTER XVIII

FROM ROME TO NOME

Alaska at Last—8,900 Miles in Less Than Two Months.

> Upon my diadem
> In filagree of frost I wear
> The Midnight Sun for a gem
> The unknown North has fingers
> That reach unto my tide
> Oh, not for balmy pleasures
> He clutches deep and wide.
>
> Oh ye, who fear not anguish
> Ye souls of steel, come forth.
> As Jacob fought with the Angel
> Come struggle with the North.
> Stan l face to face with trouble
> And meet death with a shout
> The gale that dims your courage
> Shall blow the North star out.[1]

LATE in August, 1910, Mother Amadeus left New York on her way to the Third Chapter General of the Order. She took with her some French nuns who were returning to their communities. With her usual unselfishness she tarried to look after their comfort, and thus missed an opportunity to attend the Passion Play at Oberammergau which Mother Vicar had given her permission to witness.

At the Chapter Mother Amadeus was appointed first Provincial of Alaska, with the commission to organize

[1] *The Polar Sun*, by Curtis May.

the great work in the Arctic. Joyfully did she leave Rome on September 16th. That night she took ship in Naples to reach New York six days later. On the dock she was met by her companion to Alaska, she rushed through the customs and boarded the Erie train for Chicago. Here she met two more missionaries, and was off for Seattle. The train was late. Mother Amadeus telegraphed the *Northwestern* to await her. It was the last north-bound boat of the year. At 6 P. M. that night she boarded the boat with her companions, trunks and parcels, not a mistake, not a hitch of any kind. It was a masterly piece of engineering. And on the evening of October 2d, the *Northwestern* steamed out from beneath the shadow of Mt. Ranier bearing the messengers from Rome to Nome.

Mother Amadeus was, however, well-nigh exhausted by the gigantic effort, for she had not had a breathing spell since August. Important matters at the Chapter, incessant writing in a hot, wretched cabin on the *City of Berlin*, the stretch from New York to Seattle, the incessant pain of the hip of which she took no notice, had all but broken her down. This, kindhearted Captain Croskey noticed, and he transferred Mother Amadeus from her poor cabin to the bridal chamber where he insisted she should remain in bed. All the crew, from the gentle, lady-like and refined stewardess, Miss Nellie Sullivan, to the deck boy, vied with one another and with the Captain, to do her honor, with deep true hearted kindness. It was the Alaskan tradition, beginning, the undying law of brotherhood. It was well for Mother Amadeus that she was thus surrounded. Her strength was nearly spent, and the passage was very rough. Day after day, the sea pounded against the sides of the *Northwestern* like the cannonading of an army; twice she hove to because of the merciless northern winds. The sea broke into the cabins, deluging the berths and drove the nuns out, smashing the windows and wounding the sleepers.

At length the wearying journey came to an end, and historic Nome lay smiling before us. The gallant Captain Ross of the United States life saving station lifted Mother Amadeus in his arms as gently as a mother might lift a baby—for her weight was merely nominal— from the liner to the launch and then into the dory (a flat-bottomed boat). Leaning over the side of the steamer, she had said: "I shall never get into that dangerous boat." "You bet your life you will," and she was flying in his arms to a seat in the dory, ere she was aware. Watching with the experienced eye of the skilled seaman, he caught the crest of the landward wave, and with it triumphantly bore his prize to Nome's historic beach. And a more difficult feat than a successful landing at Nome is scarcely recorded in nautical annals, for the town sprang up where Lindquist found the gold, not where convenience counseled.

The east and west point of Alaska are as far removed as the Atlantic from the Pacific. Indeed Alaska stretches its long island fingers over to Japan in the Eastern hemisphere, north and south it extends the distance of Canada from Mexico. San Francisco thus lies east of the centre of the United States and Sitka (the high land), rules in the centre. The coast line is 26,364 miles long, longer than the earth's circumference, the area 590,884 square miles, or one-sixth the area of the United States. Alaska is rich in glaciers, those frozen rivers that travel seaward at the rate of

about an inch a day, and discharge in shouting icebergs
to the sea. The most famous of these is the Malaspina with a frontage of 100 miles to the sea, the Muir
rising 1,000 feet above the sea level, and the Valdez,
fifteen miles long. The great river, highway and pro-
vider of the land is the lordly Yukon, navigable for
2,000 miles and more, receiving the Porcupine from the
north, the Tanana from the south, and bursting into
the Behring through one of the most famous of all
deltas. From the mainland, Alaska stretches out into
the Eastern hemisphere, the long line of submerged vol-
canoes, 150 in number, known to us as the Aleutian
Islands.

Alaska boasts 1,200 islands. Mt. Fairweather, Mt.
St. Elias, Mt. McKinley are its loftiest peaks. The north
is covered with "Tundra" (the Russian word for moss),
whilst in the southeast are rich lovely forests of pine,
spruce and hemlock.

The native races are three: the Eskimo (the eaters
of raw flesh), whose real name is "Innuit;" the Aleuts
or island dwellers, and the Indians; the Tineh in the
north and the Thlinkets, a decadent race stretching
from Yakutat to Puget Sound in the south. These latter
are the authors and developers of "Totemism." The
totem pole is the social directory. Dwellers beneath
the same totem may not intermarry, for the totem in-
dicates blood relationship.

The Russians were allured by the little sable into
Siberia and then across the thirty-six miles strait where
their lynx eyes dimly descried Alaska (the great country). These were the "Promishliniki," the dauntless
forerunners. The Britsh came to Alaska following
the beaver through Canada. Their land of fabulous

wealth, "The Klondike," is named from the Indian word "Thorndieck," meaning "Plenty of Fish," which to them came to mean "Plenty of Gold."

Shadows creep over the hillsides in the long Alaskan twilight, and wrap the landscape in a glamour of mystic beauty. And as day wanes, the panoply of sunset is spread athwart the gateway of the west. The land is cruel, ungracious to the Eskimo, but the sea and the river feed him. Alaska has coal, petroleum, iron, silver, lead, copper, gold, zinc, antimony, quicksilver, tin, platinum, gypsum, pete, asbestos, graphite, mica.

Paleontologists tell us—facetiously?—that the land of the long night was once a tropical jungle, inhabited by mastodons from twelve to sixteen feet in length. They point in proof of their assertions to the relics found in Arctic Alaska: tusks, bones, teeth of the mastodon, and to Maxwell's strange house built of the ribs of the pre-historic animal. In October, 1919, eighty bodies of pre-historic Eskimos were discovered under three feet of ice near Barrow, skins, dwellings and implements perfectly preserved. They say that the poles were the only points of the earth cool enough for habitation, and they place the "Garden of Paradise" at Point Barrow, averring that as the earth's crust cooled off, mankind moved in the direction of the tropics.

One of the wonders of Alaska is the famous boundary line between Alaska and Yukon, erected by the Hon. Thomas Riggs, Governor of Alaska, for 600 miles along the 141st meridian, from Mt. St. Elias, on the Pacific, to the Arctic Ocean. This gigantic avenue, which it took seven years to complete, is marked by monuments, three and four miles apart. Some of these monuments are five foot aluminum bronze shafts, set in 2,000 pounds of concrete, and others, the lesser ones, are aluminum cones set in 500 pounds of concrete. There are two hundred of these monuments along 600 miles of the straightest line engineers ever drew, going straight ahead wherever the needle pointed, regardless of obstacles or obstructions. All had to be freighted up under difficulties which stagger the imagination, but the true dividing line is there now, and there to stay.

King Island is eighty miles out from Nome. It is a rocky, storm-beaten cliff. The dwellers there lovingly climb up its rugged sides to what they call "home," the strange huts clinging to the rock and supported on stakes along the steep coast. They love it, this eyrie thrown out into the Behring Sea. They share it with unnumbered birds, with the northern winds, the frantic storms. *"Où l'amour ne va-t-il pas se nicher?"* The cloven surface of King Island admits the sea at all points, hence its people derive sufficient support such as it is. A single walrus is not to be despised, for it furnishes 1,500 pounds of meat, 1,000 pounds of oil, 500 pounds of leather. A white whale is still more valuable. So close to heaven are King Islanders, so far removed from contaminating influences and enervating luxury, that they are thoroughly good, thoroughly Catholic. The missionaries sun their weary hearts with this simple people. Once a year do the natives jump into their kayaks and go over to Nome, men, women and children, old and young, hale and sick. The dogs alone remain, and when the Islanders return after the bartering season is over, they find the animals plump and hardy as ever. The have found plentiful provender in the mollusks, the offal of the sea and air.

All the winter Islanders are busy preparing curios, furs, and skins which they barter in Nome, and, if belated in the Metropolis of the North, the Revenue Cutter *Bear* takes them home whilst Behring Sea is swept by gales and mountainous waves are thundering on the Nome beach. Our King Islanders' first care on reaching Nome is to go to the church, nor will they speak to any one, or even accept the most tempting offer of trade until they have paid homage to the King in the silent Tabernacle. They give example of sturdy honesty and truthfulness to Nome once every year, and before the stormy season sets in, they are back upon their rock for another twelvemonth. Cliff dwellers they are in every sense of the word, the only ones in North America, and there could scarcely be a less inviting dwelling on earth than theirs. Yet are these "First Christians" of Alaska the delight of the missionaries' hearts. Nevertheless, in 1910, our hearts stood still when we heard Mother Amadeus pleading, in her crippled condition, to be sent to these Islanders. It was only when the Bishop and the Superior of the Jesuits told her they had no resident priest for the Islands, that if she went, she would have Mass and the Sacraments once a year, that she desisted. For there was one sacrifice, only one, the magnanimous Ursuline would not make, would not ask us to make, and that was deprivation of the Most Blessed Sacrament. But the fact that she wanted to go to King Island, shows better than anything in her noble and wonderful life, what she was, and how she loved God and souls to the total forgetfulness of all else besides.

This circumstance fixed her at St. Michael.

CHAPTER XIX

St. Michael

GAUNT and ghoul-like, but with a weird fascination for the Russian adventurer, a long finger of land stretches out into the grim desolation of Behring Sea, North Latitude 63-33, West Longitude 161-63. "Come," it seemed to beckon. "See the world's great river, the silver horde of salmon, the masses of gold. Look at nature's majestic curve as I encircle the bay in a giant embrace. Look up at the silent stars, the loud-shrieking Aurora, the stately Mt. St. Michael in all the serenity of ice and snow."

Some such silent words must have sounded in the ears of Michael Tebenkoff when, in 1833, at the behest of the Russian Governor, Baron von Wrangell, he sat himself down on the narrow neck of land to build old Fort St. Michael, and open a trading post for the Czar of all the Russias.

They hastened to build of Alaskan cypress, brought all the way from Sitka, eleven hundred miles away, the Fort long known as Michaeloffski, the Redoubt. They builded strong and well against crashing ice and howling winds, a fort ten feet high in the form of a quadrangle with palisades between the buildings, placing there cannon cast in Russia in 1517. Then they began their forward march to wealth of furs and power, wading unscrupulously through streams of native blood and tears. Little houses built of spruce logs from the Yukon, for the Island of St. Michael offers only scrub

162

willow and low alder, began to rise about the Redoubt and to stretch along the beautiful line of the shore. For the Eskimo lives near the water for fear of the wicked inland spirits, and the goddess Famine—they are fish-eaters all of them—and the white man built as the Eskimo had builded before him. These wee homes shelter the four hundred all-year-round dwellers of St. Michael. Today it still lies caressingly about the beautiful curve of its bay, through the great Fort St. Michael from Dajek (old St. Michael), where rules Doglonak in hereditary squalor, where night and day the Kajim shelters bathers, dancers, and the tribal story-teller, to Longsite (a corruption of along side the fort), where dwell the more cultured Eskimos.

As you stand beside what now remains of the old Russian Redoubt, and look toward the bluff on the opposite side, your eye is caught by the steeple of the little Catholic church, and beyond, the silent monitors of the United States wireless station attracting into the wilderness of wind, the sparks of the world's intelligence just where St. Michael's Bay merges into Norton Sound. Beyond that again, Egg Island with its lighthouse, the first to greet the coming, the last to speed the going. It seems like the vast unknown and fills you with the terror of uncertainty. The vocal mists of the past hang over this point of land, for many distinguished travelers have passed this way and vanished, and no point on earth has been more eagerly sought or sighed for, for St. Michael is the seaport of the Behring, the link between beckoning wealth and old home loves and longings.

Upon the beach lie fastened in ice for eight months of the year the river boats that have carried much of

the world's wealth or hope of wealth—mute chroniclers
now.   Chief among these for many a month lay the
Polar Bear of Arctic fame.   This boat, a sailor with
gasoline motor, drawing ten feet and carrying 50 tons,
was left in the care of Fort St. Michael by Captain
Hadley, the greatest of the ice captains.   After living
thirty years at Point Barrow, and piloting Stefanson to
the discovery of the "Blonde Eskimo," he went outside
in 1918, only to become a victim of the influenza.   This
boat sat and brooded upon the shore like a spectre of
the past.   It beheld Victoria Land east of the mouth of
the Mackenzie, with the last undiscovered race, a race
of stalwart men, descendants of the Vikings, stranded
there and forgotten in the perennial ice and snow.
They adopted the food, the manners, the language of
the Eskimos without losing their blue eyes and yellow
hair.   The Innuits knew of them as "far away," just
as they knew of the gold hidden deep in the frozen soil,
but they pursued the even tenor of their way in traditional and stolid silence, telling naught of what they
knew, for in Alaska, as elsewhere, "discovery must be
the result of accident."

Now this adventurer slept upon our shores. And St.
Michael is radiant as fairyland in winter beauty, with
its dogs and sleds, skimming like lightning over Nature's peerless bridge.   The stars and the Aurora shine
down upon it, and the Catholic Church stands out upon
the hill, with the village of Dajek at its feet, for the
poor instinctively know where to go for comfort and
consolation.   The burying ground of the Eskimo is
there, and the God's Acre behind the church, where lie
two great Jesuits, Father Camile and Brother Paquin.

St. Michael boasts, too, a Russian Church built

forty years ago, which contains many quaint and precious pictures and vestments, and which, for many days, gave shelter to the remains of the martyred Archbishop Seghers when they were first brought down from Nulato. The bear skin upon which he died and which they also brought, was given to the American Missionary, Father Judge, S.J. One of the archimandrites was found in the ice and snow where he had perished with $60,000 worth of jewels upon his person, and with them untouched, he was carried to Unalaska for burial.

St. Michael has come to stay. There are no fresh water springs on the island, but just across the bay are medicinal waters bubbling up at temperate heat, despite the long stretches of minus forty and minus that. Here, as at Point Barrow, wells have been dug through sixty feet of ice and the thermometer often drops to sixty below and the anemometer registers ninety miles and more an hour.

The great yearly excitement here, as in all Alaskan towns, is the betting on the exact minute of the "break up." The following clipping from a Fairbanks paper will show the importance Alaskans attach to this pivotal point of their year, and better than any word of mine, gives the local color of the Alaskan white settlement.

"Under the direction of Jack Ronan, superintendent of telegraphs and telephones, the final arrangements for the registering of the official time have been made. A stake, bearing a flag has been firmly imbedded in the ice on the bosom of the river to which a taut No. 14 wire, leading to the stiff-leg derrick on the dock is attached. On the derrick on the dock there is also a switch which is connected by a wire to a bell in the upper power house, with a trip attachment from the bell of the clock.

"At the end of the taut wire leading from the stake on the ice to the stiff-leg derrick on the dock, there is a hook attached, which supports a weight attached to the handle of the switch on the derrick.

"The stake on the ice is set fifty feet upstream from the derrick, and when the ice has moved 100 feet the taut wire from the stake to the derrick will break and release the weight, which in turn will throw the switch. This will have the effect of automatically ringing the bell and stopping the clock in the power house at the same time, and the engineer who may happen to be on duty at the time will blow the whistle, which may be a second or two later than the actual time registered.

"A committee composed of H. B. Joseph, G.L. (Capt.) Hall and Harry Davis will have charge of the arrangements for registering the official time of the breakup. One of their number will probably be detailed to take entire charge of the clock in the power house and will satisfy himself daily as to its correctness. No one will be allowed to have anything to do with the clock until after the big breakup."

The natives have instincts as unfailing as the electric clock of other brains, and just at the right time they tie up their dogs for the summer rest, and make ready their kayaks. Somehow these children of nature make fewer mistakes than their science-taught brethren.

There is greatness and largeness in the whole history of Alaska. Spanish explorers from the south crept up the coast to Puget Sound, claiming as theirs the whole Southern Sea (the Pacific). Portuguese came, too, French, Italians, English, Americans, but the Russians from the opposite end, pushed down undaunted by the ferocity of the climate, despising the gold of which they knew, and eagerly seeking the more lucrative and beautiful furs. No less a man than Peter the

Great had determined upon the conquest, for he wanted
Russia to embrace the entire Arctic in the New World
as in the Old, so, with a dying hand, he traced the plan
of the expedition to the great land Alaska, which Potoff
had seen across the narrow straits. His widow carried
out his plans, and in 1741 Vitus Behring sailed across
the icy waters. Storms and misfortunes broke the
sailor's spirit with his life, and he laid him down on
the Aleutian Island that bears his name, amid the wild
vast splendors of the Alaskan Alps, so vast that Switz-
erland could easily be hidden in one of its gorges.
And when the Russian sway was firmly planted at
Sitka, by such men as Baranof and Shelikof, one of the
Governors, Baron Von Wrangell, ordered the expedition
to St. Michael, the beautiful. St. Michael is now and
ever will be the most important seaport of the Behring.
unless our provident government erects a naval base at
the so easily fortified Dutch Harbor. Thus, it would
stretch a line of defense to Honolulu, 2,000 miles in
front of San Francisco, and make attack from the Asi-
atic side impossible.

St. Michael is the key to the world's great river, the
Yukon, navigable for 2,000 miles, and more, pouring
into the sea through four giant mouths that stretch in
an area of 90 miles along the coast, at every hour one-
third more water than the Mississippi.

The Yukon is a splendid sight to see, whether in the
majesty of ice and snow or in the might of its boat-
bearing waters. It is the home of myriads of fish in
which the salmon easily leads. Hence does it feed the
land in summer, whilst in winter it remains the great
high-road to travel into the interior of Alaska. There
is no other. At Andeaffski where the delta begins, all

trees disappear, but northward your eye rejoices in a
wealth of willow, alder, cottonwood, birch, hemlock,
spruce and low fir gracing the ascending bank. Fish
is the third industry of Alaska being preceded by fur
and metal. Alaska is the "Happy Hunting Ground" of
the world's great hunters, and hither come buyers from
everywhere, even London and Leipsic before the war,
to barter with the natives: "fox—blue, black, silver,
gray, red; minks; bears; martens; wolverines; lynx;
muskrat; squirrel and hare. The sea-otter and the fur-
seal supply the pelagic fur.

When the Russian American Fur Company lost its
charter, capital turned its eyes to our furs, and with
it the wise Seward, who bought Alaska of Russia on
March 30, 1867, though the flags were not exchanged
until October 18th of the same year. Alexander II.,
retracting the steps of Peter the Great, was glad to sell
to us, lest England should point the long finger of conquest toward Siberia.

Alaska's great wealth and power lie in the Yukon.
Its history began in bloodshed and weeping as the Russians pressed on, planting the schism and a trading
post wherever they went. We turn from this orgy of
blood and cruelty. Now all is peace in Alaska. The
Stars and Stripes wave in the Arctic winds and float at
half-mast for our departed heroes. No drop of blood,
nor enemy's heel pollutes the virgin soil. The sky
alone is blood red in its wild grandeur as though the
Recording Angel had written there the orgies of the
past. And though Kipling has said: "No law of God
or man hold North of 63," the great law of human
brotherhood obtains here, and the Holy Sacrifice is daily
offered in the chapels and churches which the generous

hand of the late Mrs. Thomas Fortune Ryan—the Angel of the Most Blessed Sacrament—builded for God in the snowy wilderness.

As we look out upon the great "Outside" with its turmoil and destructive clash of class with class, we Alaskans begin to feel that, despite our many privations, we are better off. We are the "Inside" with its wondrous secrets locked from the world by the bitterness of the wind, the ferocity of the cold—cold such as Dante —with the mighty stroke of genius, placed in that bottomless pit where suffer the traitor to his friend, his country, his God. Indeed were it not for our immortal faith, there would be despair in Alaska's strange cold.

Ten miles beyond St. Michael on the island, lies Stebbins, the very heart of the Mission life. Not a white man or woman in the village. Here Father Robaut, the companion of the martyr Archbishop Seghers, rules like the Patriarch Jacob, assembling his flock, all Eskimos, every night at the sound of the bell for night prayers and for singing. So delighted were his people when he taught them to sing the act of contrition, that when he called upon them in the Sacred Tribunal for an act of sorrow, they began, each in turn, to sing it with stentorian voices.

This is St. Michael Island, with its three Eskimo villages, Dajek, Longsite, Stebbins, Fort St. Michael and the consequent white settlement, the Queen of the Yukon, the sea-port of the Behring, antedating Nome by many years, and destined to outlive it as long as the Yukon outlives the gold-diggings. It re-echoes historic footsteps as you tread. Hither came Kennicott and Dall in the interests of the Western Union, hither Lieutenant Bernard seeking the long lost Sir John Franklin,

Schwatka and others, and here came the greatest of
all, Archbishop Seghers, and here he began both his
quest for souls and his last long sleep in the old Rus-
sion graveyard, until the *Bear* conveyed the relics to
Victoria where they now rest.

A wonderful grace and blessing was it for the wind-
beaten Islands when Mother Amadeus built there
"St. Ursula's-by-the-Sea."   The little home was con-
structed in twenty days of rough boards and tar paper.
Whilst it was building Mother Amadeus lived with
one companion at the winter hotel of the "Northern Commercial Company," and sent two others to the
"isolation hospital" to care for the children who had
all come down with the measles.   She walked every
day along the beautiful shore to the church where our
dear friend, Rev. Father Chapdelaine said Mass, and
the future martyr, Brother Paquin, served.   Often, too,
the kind Father came down to the hotel and said Mass
in Mother Amadeus' room, transformed into a chapel
by her skillful and loving hands.

On the first Friday of November, 1910, the convent
was ready and the first Mass was celebrated before the
admiring Eskimos in a chapel so sweet and prayerful
that the Bishop used to call it "My little Cathedral,"
The hand of God made it still more beautiful on the
first Christmas night.   Mother Amadeus mushed over
to Midnight Mass in a dog sled.   The pretty church was
only a few steps removed, but the snow and ice covered ground was unsafe for her cane.   After the sacred
solemnity was over, I walked pensive beside her and
our boy "Nick" the musher (driver)—mush is a corruption of the French word *marchons*.   "Look!" suddenly said Mother Amadeus.   I raised my eyes, and

beheld the Aurora in all its incandescent splendor. The dancing lights had gathered into one broad semi-circle of gold, enclosing our cabin, "St. Ursula's-by-the-Sea." It stood in the centre of all this celestial splendor as though God said: "Look! Look at the beloved of My heart who has left all to follow Me in labor and privation."

Often, often, after that night we beheld the shrieking splendor of the northern sky, the sun-dogs, the moon-dogs, the mysterious rainbow of the moon, but never with the symbolism of that first Christmas night.

All St. Michael gathered about Mother Amadeus. The winter broke intensely cold and stormy. The anemometer was running 90 miles an hour at the wireless station when it was smashed, and no further record could be kept. The furious wind that had smashed it was also tearing off the tar paper from the tiny cabin that stood out upon the bluff behind the church, and the green lumber was shrinking so that we could have slipped our hands between the boards on those dreadful nights, when our poor walls seemed the strings of some wild aeolian harp upon which the winds kept singing their weird melodies.

Often during that first winter, we sat up all night asking God to save us, for we feared we would be dashed into the Behring as other cabins were. Mother had chosen the coldest corner of the dormitory for herself, and one of her feet was frozen. It was so cold that we had to wear our "Parkees" (fur coats, seamless and slipped on over the head) all night. We could not make a fire for the wind was so high and the price of coal still higher. How to dress in the morning was a grave problem, for pins and clothing fell out of our benumbed hands. Mother Amadeus, in her heroic charity, solved the problem. She would rise before the appointed time, make her way down into the chapel before the rest, and soon equable warmth diffused throughout the little cabin. Yet she could not take a step without her cane.

On January 27th Brother Paquin was lost. He had come to St. Michael just three days before us, had served us so graciously, so generously that he reminded us of St. John Berchmans, and his angelic countenance was not unlike that of St. Stanislaus that smiled on our chapel walls. In his Novitiate days he had prayed for the grace of martyrdom; he had been the first to discover the remains of Father Arnault, the martyr, and had distinguished himself from the first day of his religious life by his energy and fervor. Our Lord knows what He wants of His own. He has made them.

The pathetic story of his early death was told by Mother Amadeus of the Heart of Jesus in a letter written by her at the time. No one can tell it better.

St. Ursula by the Sea.

St. Michael, Alaska, March 4, 1911.

DEAR EDITOR: We were deeply touched to find you had published our appeal. You do not know how kind it was of you to do so. Thank you, dear friends! *The Tidings* of December and January have reached this distant point, and the mail carriers and the dogs that brought them camped many nights in the snow.

Too experienced are they to fight these fearful Arctic storms, so dogs and men dig down into the snow and sleep there till the fury of the wind is spent.

There is a little convent, thrown up in twenty days, of green lumber and tar paper, sitting 'neath the sleepless polar star, and rocked by the wild waves of Behring Sea.

Three times a day do the sounds of Our Lady's office

ascend to heaven in choir chanted, and as the gracious ear bends towards earth, she catches this the highest, *i.e.*, the most northern note of her praise, for none other in the Arctics are chartered by rule to pay her this sweet homage.

It was in this wee cabin, all decked in snow and icicles without, but hanging peace and joy within, that your paper came, and through your kind eyes we looked upon the great, the beautiful "outside." It was comforting to grasp your hand and to know that it is linking us with so much that is good and noble in our far-away country.

Had we a particular need of the solace just now?

Three deaths have visited us, and blizzards and hurricanes, the fiercest the Arctics know, have been succeeding one another with a speed of sixty, seventy, ninety miles an hour. Our house sways and trembles in their dread embrace, so that we often hasten to the chapel to beg our Sacramental Lord's protection. Snow piles up within and without, cutting off all vision and throbbing and trembling as though lightning were flashing through it.

We greatly need your help to buy lumber to make our house habitable before another winter, and now is the time to order it that we may have it ready to begin by the opening of our short summer. But lumber which with you costs from sixteen to twenty dollars a thousand, is worth from sixty to seventy dollars here.

Many have been frozen at St. Michael this winter, and more than one noble life has been lost.

On the morning of January 27th, before the storm had begun here, Brother Ulrich Paquin of the Society of Jesus, started out with a sled, five dogs and a light load of lumber. He was going to Stebbins, a village ten miles off, where the Rev. Jesuit Fathers are building a chapel for the natives. Stebbins is attractive to the missionary heart. It lies at the western extremity of St. Michael Island, and is peopled by Innuits only, who live in a wonderful fraternity, and seem to have realized the ideal of true Christian communities. Nothing troubles them, for they know they will want neither food nor clothing whilst there is a native at St. Michael.

Brother Paquin had often traveled the road before, and on this fair morning he started out in the reindeer "parkee" and "mucklucks"—garments worn by all in this northern latitude—but without "sleeping bag" or blankets. No one could suspect that this was to be his last journey.

Out upon the tundra, the wind blew a gale at the rate of ninety miles an hour, and the snow whizzed so madly about that when within two miles of his destination, the young Jesuit lost his bearings and began his last dread battle.

He unloaded his lumber and went on a few feet to the brow of the hill, as he thought toward, but in reality away from, the Innuit village. Not seeing it, casting about in vain, buffeted by the sharp, cold wind, bewildered in the pathless snow, beguiled at length by the treacherous Arctic sleep, he lay him down upon his sled like "a warrior taking his rest, with his martial cloak about him." Consternation and sorrow reigned here when he did not return, and a diligent search was instituted for the missing Brother.

The Eskimos risked their lives in the fearful storm to save his, but it was decreed otherwise, and for a week the winds piled up the snowdrifts and kept their secret.

We still had some lingering hope, for the dogs had not come back, and these Eskimo dogs always gnaw away at the harness and come back, to give the clue. Wild, voracious, they fall upon and tear one another to pieces as soon as the guiding hand is stilled. This we knew, therefore we hoped that the Brother was awaiting in some village the cessation of the storm. At length, just one week later, the sun came out for a few hours, and two Catholic Indians found the holy corpse sleeping on the hillside. Peter, from Stebbins, the strongest man on the island, lifted it upon his back and started for St. Michael, but he had scarcely gone two miles when he was met by the government team of eleven dogs, which Captain H. F. Dalton, U. S. A., commanding officer of Ft. St. Michael, had sent to the rescue with his best "musher"—musher is a Canadian word, corrupted from *"Marchons,"* "let us go—and is used in Eskimo to designate the driver of a dog team. The five skeleton dogs followed, howling their Mahlamute dirge, and thus the weird funeral procession brought the Jesuit back to the church, toward three o'clock in the afternoon, with Peter the "Christopher."

Had the fierce dogs, despite their long fast, the bitter cold, the wild storm, kept guard all that snowy week without food or shelter—held by the frozen hand, the silent lips, the drooping eye? All St. Michael mourned and wondered. It is unwritten in Mahlamute record that famished dogs ever respect a corpse, but we do read in Saints lore of the power of sanctity over the brute creation.

At all events, what was mortal of Ulrich Paquin, S. J., was brought back unmutilated, untouched, and lay frozen to adamant in the church. Keeping his "vigil of arms" in the beautiful attitude of the dying St. Stanislaus at St. Andrea del Quirinale in Rome. The same smile upon the marble lips—the presence of God and trust in Him written in stone upon the young and open brow, the rosary frozen upon his "parkee" somewhere near his lips, as though his last conscious act in the bewildering storm had been to press it reverently, "Now and at the hour of our death." And the Lady "Ad Nives" must have stood beside him in his agony. For God keeps His own and His mighty arm soon snatched the young religious from the relentless Arctic storm, and laid him down to sleep whilst his Virgin Mother stood beside him. That night an Eskimo boy nailed the rude coffin and we sat up to line and cover it, and the next morning we sang the Requiem Mass. But the furious winds had arisen in the meantime and kept the body with us four days longer, when another lull and another bit of sunshine allowed the Father to lay him away in the frozen God's Acre, where, in adamantine incorruption, he awaits the summoning blast to the last great meeting. St. Michael is an iceberg.

Brother Ulrich Paquin, S.J., had been eleven years in the order. Born of a very good family of St. Didau, Province of Quebec, Canada, he was full of vigor, activity, energy, kindness.

The Mission never wanted anything while he, its ministering angel, lived. His strong arm brought us coal and ice

—for in winter there is no water in Alaska—as though they were only a featherweight, and served us from the Father's residence with untiring charity. Oh, but the Brother knew how to do things quickly, quietly and well. Obedience was his shining mark, and beautiful, beautiful was this obedience in its strong faith and trust. Though he had reached St. Michael only three days before we did, the reputation of his sanctity had penetrated his mask of silence and retirement, and all, we above all, are lamenting his sudden going forth from our midst; and his spirit still lingers about our little chapel where he served Mass with angelic modesty and devotion. He is the first member of the great Order to meet with a violent death in Alaska, and St. Michael venerated him for his fidelity to duty.

Sainted Ulrich Paquin, S.J., rest thou in peace! Ah, it is a strange land, wild and weird, this frozen north, and God is ever teaching mighty lessons.

Again the funeral bell tolled from the little steeple, and Sergeant Dalton, U. S. A., was brought within the compass of the church's soothing "requiems."

An Ursuline played the strains of Beethoven's pathetic march, as Captain Dalton, U. S. A., all the officers, and companies M and D of the 16th Infantry, filed into the little white and blue church and took their seats upon the benches beside the man who lay asleep in the flag.

And how fit it seemed that those brave men, and the noblest flag the winds of earth do know, should rest awhile in the arms of the Catholic Church, the house of the God that dieth not, the mother of all things splendid and beautiful. United States soldiers listened reverently to the "Subvenite," the "Libera," the "In Paradisum"—the time-honored Gregorian that has laid the world's noblest spirits to rest, and then filed through the church doors that opened wide upon the frozen Behring.

Sergeant Dalton paused for the last time on the threshold he loved so well. Before him lay the beautiful curve of St. Michael's shore, iridescent in winter's magnificence, and beyond the sea that cut him off from all that he had loved in life. At a given signal the firing squad of sixteen men, eight from each company, fired a volley over the corpse into the sea. Again! hark! again! Then rang out the taps clear and solemn for the last time for the Catholic soldier, and the funeral line marched on over the snow back to Ft. St. Michael.

And as the regular thud, thud and tramp fell upon our ears, another funeral procession, hastily gathered together and headed by Rev. J. Chapdelaine, S.J., and the cross bearer, hurried off to the little God's Acre where Brother Paquin lay waiting them. A poor consumptive Indian boy, whom he and the Father had nursed with angelic patience and charity, and to whom the latter had brought Holy Communion every day since Christmas—we had sung the "Dies Irae" in the morning—followed by his sorrowing mother, was carried away to burial, and St. Michael's air was vocal again with God's mysterious mighty lessons. Two funeral processions together—the soldier's with all the pomp and ceremony that the flag doth lend, and the poor Indian—a staggering, wailing line lifted up by the emblems of the Divine—both diverging from the one focus to different points, and each speaking its message to desolate St. Michael.

But there is a bright side to the picture—our little children, who manifest such great delight in coming to the convent to be taught. Already have they learned the "Missa de Angelis," which they are to sing on St. Joseph's day. They do so with sweet simplicity and devotion, and I sometimes think that our Holy Father would be pleased to catch strains of their obedience here at the antipodes. Their greatest punishment would be not to be taught, and their sweet innocence is the delight and consolation of our present life. Wondrously weather-wise and cunning to fight the elements are they, with senses and instincts keenly developed. They come in furs and leggings made of the fore-leg of the reindeer, all quite impervious to wind and cold. They loiter about in the snow and stand gazing at the frozen sea with the delight with which our boys and girls at home stretch themselves out 'neath the apple trees. But there are no snowballs here, for the snow is too fine, too dry, and all is meditative and silent.

The wind alone has a voice as it rocks the little cabin.

Coal is twenty-five dollars undelivered and thirty dollars when brought by the only horse on the island, and the cold is relentless for eight months of the year.

So, dear friends, we thank you for remembering us, and our children, and beg you still to do so in the golden charity of your hearts; and not mightier are these words than is the voice of our gratitude ascending in prayer from our hearts to where are Peace and Love.

We do thank you who have remembered us, and beg your dear hands to lend themselves now to the completion of our cabin before another dreadful winter sets in, for we have to go about sweeping out the snow and catching the dripping water while stiff breezes and joint benumbing cold come in through the rifts of this poor little hut.

You may think of us beginning our daily toils many hours before the dawn, for the winter sun arises at 10 A. M., and sets at 2 P. M. Beginning then with prayer for you in our chapel where we have daily Mass and Holy Communion. It is truly wonderful that you can reach us where we are locked in by ice and snow. Comforting that we can reach and help you in the dear Sacred Heart of Jesus.

Our mail is necessarily slow, so great are the distance and the difficulties, and it has been calculated that a letter which costs you two cents to send, costs Uncle Sam one dollar to deliver. Navigation is closed and the dogs cannot carry heavy loads, so each point of the trail has a certain percentage of mail apportioned to it according to the population. For which reason St. Michael gets but little. Moreover, the selection is arbitrary, and of two letters leaving the States together, one might go through in fifty days, and the other lie over until the next delivery. Then, too, the trail softens and becomes impassable before the ice goes out to sea and river, and when this happens letters are arrested at St. Michael and Nome, the northern, and Valdez and Cordova, the southern termini, and kept over for the first north-bound steamer, which cannot get in till the

MOTHER AND NUNS ON CONVENT GROUNDS, VALDEZ.

middle of June at the earliest. So there must necessarily come a lull, but all is safe and we shall unfailingly write whenever we hear from you. Let us send to each one our thanks in advance. Breathing the blessing of the old Gael, "May thy open hands be filled the fullest."

In great and sincere gratitude,

SUPERIOR OF URSULINES OF ALASKA.

Money reaches us safe by check, registered letter or money order on postoffice, St. Michael, Alaska, made out to Sister Mary Amadeus.

St. Ursula's-by-the-Sea, by its position, commanded a splendid view of the Behring at the point where the St. Michael Bay merges into Norton Sound. We were the first to see the boats coming, the last to see them going. It was a delight to us, too, to hail the stout little *Corwin* as she came ploughing in through the ice the first of all the boats on St. Angela's day, May 31st. To know the meaning of such expressions as "First Boat," "Last Boat" you must have wintered in Alaska. We used to watch, too, the almost midnight sun as it dropped beneath the waves trailing its line of light along the horizon, and, visible all the way, re-appeared in regal splendor twenty minutes after.

CHAPTER XX

AKULURAK—VALDEZ

In August came the *St. Joseph*, the Mission boat, on its yearly quest for freight. Manned by the Jesuits and their boys, it meets the first ocean steamer at St. Michael every season, then goes threading its way up the lordly Yukon until it has left the yearly supply of provisions at each mission. For some of these the visit of the *St. Joseph* is the only link with civilization, and what it does not bring, cannot come for another twelvemonth.

The *St. Joseph* brought Bishop Crimont, Fathers Lucchesi, Peron and Treca with Mother Laurentia and one of the Eskimo girls from St. Mary's mission to St. Ursula's-by-the-Sea. The Jesuits wept when they saw the state of our cabin, and they determined to make it safe against another winter. They sent to Nome for the carpenter Brother that he might do this work, but, in the meantime, Father Treca, who was to play so important a part in our lives, urged that we all go up and spend the winter at Akulurak. The eloquence of his life more than of his words prevailed. Hastily we packed into bags our few belongings, and off we started on the *St. Joseph*.

The little floating convent broke from its moorings on August 13, 1911, and on August 15th at about 1 P. M. it stopped at St. Mary's Mission. We had had two Masses every morning and at Nunapikluga (Old Fort Hamilton) Rev. Father Treca had baptized a boy, naming him Amadeus after the saintly guest of the

180

boat. We had shot ducks on our way, and stopped often to let down the missionary as the opportunity for good arose. On one such occasion, the Father went to bless a marriage. The Eskimo was in one corner of the church, but the bride? Where was she? The good shepherd left the altar to seek the most necessary adjunct to the ceremony. He found her in the kitchen making pancakes for the wedding breakfast. "Oh!" said the astonished and blushing bride, "I thought you could do it without me." At night the *St. Joseph* cast anchor that the crew might sleep, and so we went meandering on our way to the Akulurak River. This tortuous stream empties into one of the arms of the Yukon in the vast delta. It is dotted, here and there, with an Eskimo village. Never a white woman has set her foot in the labyrinth. There are no white people there at all save the Jesuits and the Ursulines. But nestled in the forty-eighth bend of the pretty stream, lies St. Mary's Mission, the very oasis of peace. Difficult and inconvenient to reach is the blessed Mission, yet the Fathers were obliged to locate where they did because the vicinity of the United States Bird Reserve, the river, the fish, the fur, make it a desirable spot for our people. Mother Amadeus' arrival at this "the end of the world," was the cause of the greatest joy to nuns, children and the Innuits, and there she remained from August 15, 1911, to June 10, 1912.

As Provincial, in 1905, with the permission obtained at the first Chapter General, Mother Amadeus had opened this blessed Mission. Her nuns had worked there wonders of unselfish devotion. Already had they begun to gather in the little ones of the second generation. They did all they could to make Mother Amadeus' stay a happy one, and they succeeded. This year was the happiest of her long and fruitful missionary career. How she gloried in the northern lights that were always playing fantastic tricks out upon the sky! How uplifted was her soul by these beauties of the heavens.

She quickly won the hearts of the little Innuits. Her smile was enough. They soon learned the way to her room and seldom did she enjoy the luxury of being alone. Our annual retreat that year was given by Father Treca. It was the most beautiful, the most wonderful we had ever known. During the retreat, kind Father Chiavassa, the Superior, performed the duties of Prefect.

After this retreat, the poor poured into the little parlor adjoining Mother Amadeus' room, in unwonted numbers. She was much surprised. But she had said one day to the children: "Dear children, I love you so well, that I wish I had been born at Akulurak that I might never be obliged to leave you." These words flew up and down the river, and the people came to the Fathers saying: "Show us the Mother who loves the Innuits."

Every day the great scholar, Father Treca, used to teach catechism in Innuit, and we were allowed to assist and absorb what we might of his wonderful lore.

In one of her missionary trips, Mother Amadeus had met Father Barnum. These true-hearted, great missionaries understood each other at a glance. The Jesuit had left his mark in Alaska, and impressed all by the broadness, the largeness of his views, his boundless generosity. Stationed at Tununa and Akulurak in the early days of their unspeakable desolation, he set himself to the giant task of learning the Innuit language. Difficult at best would be this task in a well-appointed university with light and heat and all the modern appliances of comfort—books and professors at hand. But at Cooper Bay, in a cold cabin, with insufficient food, a seal oil-lamp and a non-commital Eskimo for sole professor—it was a gigantic work. Father Barnum has amusingly recorded how he often learned a word at the risk of losing his hands, for often on a missionary trip he heard the desired syllable just in the context that was most clear, at last, and he would pull off his mittens, then and there, to take notes, fearing all the while that his hands would be frozen. Father Barnum's work on the "Fundamentals of Innuit" has elicited the praise of the learned. The Innuit language, he tells us, is a complex of the highest degree, and differs from all the Aryan languages. Many and various are the modes of expression and slight are the differences between the words. Polysynthetic, the nouns have 230 variations, and the verbs still more. One verb is capable of 700 tense endings. For instance: I walk, I walk fast, I can or cannot walk, are all expressed by tense endings of the same verb. Out of this multiplicity and complexity come fixed forms for every idea, and great clearness and precision at last. Such a sentence as "He gave him his hat," whether John's hat or Sam's, given to John or to Sam, is impossible in Innuit, and Innuit land is probably the only one under the sun where a mistake in grammar is never heard. Men, women and children, all speak with absolute correctness. But all this complex lucidity is an additional toil for our heroic priests, who, in loneliness, darkness, cold, and unimagined privations, unravel the mystery, and succeed in playing on the instrument of the Innuit language, the sweet music of God's message of salvation.

Signagtugag is a story written in Eskimo by one M. Storch, son of a Greenland whale hunter, and Father Barnum has succeeded in perpetuating in print the stories that the tribal "Story-Teller" drones out morning and evening to our people. His dignity is hereditary, second only to that of the Chief. He is the town clock. He wakens the sleepers in the "Kajim" in the morning, and his droning puts them to sleep at night. He may not change a word of the stories as he tells them day after day.

On November 25th we had just assembled in the refectory for supper, when violent knocking was heard at the door. It was the feast of our second Patroness, St. Catherine of Alexandria, the snow was deep, the cold bitter. We opened. Johnnie from St. Michael stood there with his dogs and his sled. He brought a dispatch from Bishop Crimont, telling Mother Amadeus to come to Valdez as soon as possible to open a house where support was assured. The messenger had spent a week in coming, and charged only $50 for the delivery of this dispatch.

"Soon" proved to be June 6th, earnestly as Mother Amadeus desired to obey the summons. There could be no question of travel for the river was frozen from St. Ursula's day to St. Angela's day. And our blessed life ran on. On Christmas night the kind Father sent up, to the children's inexpressible wonder and delight, the fireworks offered them by a kind benefactor for July 4th. But as July 4th is the high light of the long day, they kept the celebration for Christmas. The children used to sit complacently in the snow and draw pictures of Innuit life with a long pointed wooden or ivory knife provided for that purpose. Their great delight was to fry pancakes in seal oil, a process that had to take place out of doors for obvious reasons. On big days, they had their picnics out upon the frozen river and in their parkees they defied the coldest cold. Then they would gather in the evenings about the beautiful bright coal oil lamp in the recreation room they loved so well, and work like fairies in wampun and basketry. Happy indeed were they, not caring for the comforts, the wonders they knew not of in the great "Outside." How sweetly they sang in the chapel and in the church, both in Innuit and in English. How they loved the "canned music" (the phonograph), kind and generous Father Treca used to bring over on feast days. And every afternoon he would sit in the sacred tribunal and listen as one might listen to embryo Theresas. Few among our dear children were not daily communicants, and when sadness stole into their little hearts, the little feet would carry them into the chapel very close to the Tabernacle. For everything the Jesuits and Ursulines had or knew was theirs.

Often the Father and the nuns were surprised by gifts from the tribe when one of the big feasts was on: a new parkee, a blubber of seal oil, (we had a special outdoor shed for this Innuit luxury), a dish of akutak. This is their ice-cream, delicately fashioned, daintily served by these graceful, unconscious children of nature. And Mother Amadeus would have to taste this, to them, delightful tidbit, and then offer it to them saying: "Now this is so good, my little girl must eat it herself," and she would skip off delighted, quite un-

conscious that she was doing something Mother could
not possibly do.

On June 6th, whilst she was making ready to go
to meet the Bishop of Valdez, Mother Amadeus heard
an ominous sound, a dreadful rumbling. She wondered, yet continued her preparations for departure
though the engineer Brother said it was altogether too
soon to venture down the river. It was only after she
reached Valdez that Mother knew that she had heard
the muffled roar of Katmai in eruption. This cataclysm
has been ever since a study to scientists. They have
calculated that had the eruption taken place at Vesu-
vius, the rumbling would have been heard in Paris,
and Rome would have been covered with ashes. As it
was, all Alaska was disturbed, the United States Ex-
perimental Station on the Island of Kodiak was ruined,
and all the cattle perished. The ashes of the monster
volcano were everywhere, and all that year the clouds
that overhung the sky were attributed to the Katmai
eruption.

It evidently did disturb the Kwislak (one of the
branches of the Yukon), for when Mother reached it,
the tiny launch *St. Mary* could not venture into its trou-
bled waters. We were obliged to turn back to the dear
Mission, to the delight of nuns and children, and await
the 10th of June when Mother made a second attempt
to reach Valdez. With her went her companion, Mary
Claver, an Innuit girl, the engineer Brother, and Father Treca. This last act of exquisite courtesy enabled
her to have Holy Mass every day of that eventful
journey to the Yukon. This time she reached "Nunapikluga" (Old Hamilton), on the great Yukon. As the
St. Mary entered the giant stream, the sun—it was mid-

night—emerged from its feint of descent below the
horizon. How beautiful it was! How beautiful Mother
Amadeus' countenance in the celestial radiance! The
silence was intense. It invited to prayer. Suddenly
a voice broke the sublime stillness. "Kahlekat" called
a boy from the opposite side of the stream. He was
returning from St. Michael with the mail, and seeing
the Mission boat, he stopped us to deliver it in mid-
Yukon.

The Innuit word means letters. The Father understood. He boarded the fishing smack, for stretched
upon the tiny deck was a sick man whom he comforted.
Is not the Alaskan life beautiful and wonderful! And
how these Fathers went about scattering hope broad-
cast with truth. The Sacred Heart of Jesus was making
use of them to redeem His own great twelfth promise.
At times like these, deprivations and discomfort grow
more entrancing than all the world knows of comfort
and luxury.

Mother Amadeus sought refuge in the school-house
with her companion and our Eskimo girl, whilst the
two Jesuits occupied the room back of the church.
This little church is one of the many built by the late
Mrs. Thomas Fortune Ryan. Every morning whilst we
waited for the boat, we had Mass and Holy Communion. Were we not to be envied? How few, even of
the wealthiest Catholics, travel with a chaplain? But
you see, we Alaskans are princesses of the Church. We
taste these luxuries.

Old Hamilton is only a flagging station. So one of
our boys sat night and day out upon the roof of the
schoolhouse to hail the big boat lest it might slip down
the river unawares. Though the beds were very hard

—boards and no mattress, still the week we waited was
one of spiritual delights. Our people poured into the
schoolhouse. They begged Mother Amadeus to stay
and open school. How gladly would she have done so!
The village is genuine Eskimo. Dark eyed children
tumbled about with their dogs in and about their
cabins, under fish-racks, behind the fish caches, into
the kayaks and out of them, whilst the men plied the
fishing nets and the women mended them, and the great
stream flowed majestically on: to the Pagan eye, a
protecting deity, in his splendor yielding food in lavish
abundance, to the Christian, the manifestation of an
exuberant and benign Providence.

Nunapikluga with Mother Amadeus, Father Treca
and our children was the high light of Mission life. A
week sped swiftly by, and the huge thing of fire and
smoke bore down upon us—the *Susie* the river boat
bound for St. Michael and the outside. For to go to
Valdez, Mother Amadeus was obliged to return to
Seattle, and there take ship for southwestern Alaska.
There is no other way of communication in the monster land.

Our boy rushed in one morning calling "Balakluta,"
the boat. We had but the time to snatch our parcels,
Mother Amadeus her cane, (her cross) and reverent
hands lifted and helped her down the steep plank and
on to the *Susie*. The purser, an old friend of hers at
St. Michael, laughed and said: "How did you ever get
stranded here, Mother?" Upon the *Susie* were many distinguished travelers. Among these a buyer of furs
from Berlin, laden with pelts bartered from our people. He had even offered Father Treca $100 for the
blanket of muskrat our children had fashioned for him.

But what cared Father Treca, for money? He needed the covering given him by his children.

Mother Amadeus reached St. Michael just in time to make the *Umatilla* which was even then steaming for the "Outside." The trip south was uneventful. We were surprised and annoyed by the darkness at night to which we were no longer accustomed in the summer months. Captain Reilly was most gracious and kind. A little one was born on the trip. The baby became the general pet, and was promised the name "Mary Amadeus Umatilla Reilly."

In Seattle Mother Amadeus caught the *Alameda* and steamed out for Valdez on the feast of Our Lady of Mt. Carmel. On that day, she was the guest of Alexander McDougall who had founded Seattle Carmel for his daughter Mother Cyril, the Sub-Prioress, and the nuns there became sponsors for the new foundation, the Ursuline Convent of Valdez. On the boat Mother Amadeus again became the centre of attraction. At table one day, the waiter brought her a gift for the Missions with the following note from a Protestant gentleman, a stranger: "To the Rev. Mother, the lady whose smile is a benediction, whose benign face mirrors the eternal spirit of the living God."

We sailed through some of the world's most exquisite scenery. The Wrangell Narrows, like the fiords of Norway, threading in and out of pinegirt cliffs; Seymour Narrows, with the treacherous "Ripple Rock," the siren Acculta, who, the natives say, sings ruin and destruction there; the village of the dead, with its mute totem poles the living have abandoned; Cape St. Elias, Mt. Fairweather in their silent sublimity; the snow-clad Malaspina, Lapeyrouse, and finally Cordova on Prince

William Sound, the wonderful Valdez Narrows, with the snow-clads dropping sheer into the blue bay, a bay deep enough to harbor the United States fleet when one by one the batleships are admitted through the Narrows into the most northern United States harbor that is open all year round.

All these marvels Mother Amadeus delighted in as she sped up from Seattle to Valdez on Prince William Sound. Here in a frame convent, surrounded by lofty and beautiful trees, she found her child and friend Mother Mary of the Angels who had preceded her there with three companions on April 16th, and one more Ursuline Convent was founded by the great Mother Amadeus of the Heart of Jesus. When Very Rev. Father Crimont met her, he who had spent $50 on the preceding November to say: "Come as soon as possible," said in surprise, on July 22, 1912: "Already!" For he was a true Alaskan, and knew it was indeed a feat to reach Valdez on Prince William Sound by St. Mary Magdalen's Day.

CHAPTER XXI

Back and Forth Between Seattle and Alaska

Mother Amadeus' stay at Valdez was of short duration. All was going well. She left the house in the care of Mother Mary of the Angels, a nun of tried prudence and virtue, and she felt she could begin the great work of her life—the opening of a Novitiate for Alaska. This grace was vouchsafed her. In the year 1914, on August 23d, the fiftieth anniversary of her profession, she opened, in Seattle, with six novices, the first Alaskan Novitiate. And on that great day, she had the unspeakable joy and consolation of sending two more zealous workers up to the Mission on the Akulurak. Events crowded now upon the last years of her holy life.

The first house in Seattle was a rented one, No. 720 30th Avenue, north, but it proved unsanitary. It stood high above Lake Washington and commanded a splendid view, not only of the lake, but also of Seattle's tutelary deity, Mt. Ranier. But in spite of these great advantages it had to be given up. Moisture seeped in through the walls, and the novices were losing their health. So Mother Amadeus began to look around for other quarters in the beautiful "Spirit City."

In the meantime, Mother Vicar had come from Rome. Mother Amadeus had escorted her and her companion, Mother Evangelista, about the beautiful Montana Missions, and obtained her approval of her plans for the Alaskan work, and above all for its Novitiate. They were filled with wonder at all that had been accomplished, and left Mother Amadeus, blessing God who had done such wonderful things through her instrumentality.

Mother Amadeus' eye had long been attracted by a pretty house going up on the hill near the park, in the residence district of Mt. Baker. With eighteen rooms it looked out, from a wilderness of trees upon Mt. St. Helen's Place, and back upon McClellan Street. It was a very paradise of peace and beauty. With the permission of His Lordship Bishop O'Dea of Seattle, with her unwavering confidence in Providence, Mother Amadeus of the Heart of Jesus bought the property. She was a genius in business as well as in sanctity, and she felt, with St. Teresa, that a beautiful view is an essential part of a complete convent, a convent especially for those who were making ready to go out into the wilds of Alaska. Seattle's most distinguished business men upheld her. All wondered at this missionary from desolate Alaska who could command the most difficult situations. She won, after ten minutes' conversation, their full confidence. She was the same Sister Mary Amadeus of whom Mother Alphonsus of Toledo had said: "All I have to do is to stand Sister Amadeus out on the street corner, and she will attract all the children of Toledo."

As the district was an exclusively residence district, Mother Amadeus agreed not to open a school there, but to send her nuns down into the Italian Parish to teach. His Lordship, the Rt. Rev E. J. O'Dea was happy to give the Most Blessed Sacrament a trysting place in the only quarter of his episcopal city where the Lord had never been suffered to enter. Yet he feared legal trouble, and he asked Mother Amadeus if she were willing to take the responsibility. Fearlessly she answered that she was. Mrs. Thomas Fortune Ryan paid for this property. Soon, however, Mr. James Burke, a distinguished real estate power in Seattle died, and his restraining hand removed, "the Hunter Tract Improvement Company" brought suit. Mr. Burke had threatened that, if they disturbed "The Mother," he would break up their restrictions, but they no longer feared him. But another friend arose, Mr. James Kane of the firm of Farrel, Kane & Stratton, and, twice sued, once in the Superior Court of Seattle, and once in the Supreme Court of the State in Olympia, Mother Amadeus was twice victorious.

Mr. Kane's masterly arguments silenced forever all objectors, who soon were won over by the gentle magnetism of "The Mother." And then the God of Peace came to Seattle Ursuline Convent in the daily exposition of the Most Blessed Sacrament, and Mother Amadeus felt that her life was over, and that now she might sing her *"Nunc dimittis, Domine."* One thing still remained for her to do, and she did it.

In 1915, Mother Amadeus had gone up with her companion as a guest on the *S. S. Senator,* to visit her nuns at Akulurak. But storms so violent followed the boat that Captain Guptil would not allow her to land. Indeed, she was too ill to do so, she could not rise out of her narrow berth where she lay for thirty days. The *Senator* faced about, and when finally it reached Seattle, after one of the stormiest passages on its record, we lifted Mother Amadeus off the boat, and carried her back to Mt. Baker Park. Was her courage broken? We shall see. The return of the *Senator* to Seattle made quite a stir, for on board were one hundred and six Alaskan dogs bought by the French Government for service in the Vosges Mountains. They had boarded the boat at Nome, and the courts had adjourned, the schools, the places of business had been closed to see these winners of the "All Alaska Sweepstake" go off to the war. They were led by Captain Haas who had come all the way from France to buy them, and by the renowned "Scotty Allen," the great winner in many of Alaska's races. The dog race from Nome to Candle and back, once a year, together with the betting on the exact second of the "Break Up," form the great winter excitement of Alaska's white population. The great war dogs had thus accompanied Mother Amadeus on her fourth home trip from northern Alaska. She went in 1907, in 1910, in 1912, in 1915, in 1916, in 1918. Faithfully and generously indeed had this great Ursuline filled her duty as Provincial, and great had been the consolation, help and encouragement to nuns and children in the north. To understand what these six trips to northern Alaska meant of suffering and privation is not possible to one who has never faced the frantic northern Pacific, with the poor accommodations offered to travelers there. One great earthly joy Our Lord still had to offer His courageous Spouse.

On July 25, 1917, the Very Rev. R. J. Crimont, S.J., her last great Bishop friend, was consecrated in Seattle Cathedral, first Bishop of Alaska. He had filled the post of Prefect Apostolic of the North for nine years, with wonderful self-sacrifice and devotion, but now the crown so long deserved was placed upon his brow. The vast Prefecture of Alaska was raised to the dignity of a Vicariate, and the incumbent, the Very Rev. R. J.

Rt. Rev. J. R. Crimont, S.J., First Bishop of Alaska.

Crimont, S.J., was consecrated Bishop of Ammadera, I. P. I. Archbishop Christie of Portland, assisted by Bishop O'Dea of Seattle and Bishop Shinner of Spokane, crowned his saintly brow with the plenitude of the sacred priesthood. The evening before he had come up to see Mother Amadeus, his old friend in the frozen fields of their mutual apostolate, and he invited her to the consecration, bringing her a beautiful ceremonial of the holy rite. So, with the blessing of Bishop O'Dea, Mother Amadeus and the professed nuns then in Seattle went to the great consecration. From the pulpit they heard the decree of Pope Benedict XV., releasing the Jesuit from his vow to accept no ecclesiastical dignity, and ordering him to accept the Bishopric of Ammadera, I. P. I. They heard the bulls erecting Alaska into a Vicariate and their hearts greatly rejoiced. Above all, they received that first blessing of one whom they had long venerated as their Bishop when he went about like the humblest of the missionaries, saving, helping, comforting, guiding. Every inch did he look the Bishop on this, the day of his consecration, as though he had never been other than the "Bishop of the North Pole."

In 1918, though already attacked by her last illness, the heroic Mother Amadeus undertook another trip to Alaska. She was smiling when we lifted her from her little room in the Seattle Convent to the *Victoria*. Her dearest friends, Mrs. M. Donahoe and the Misses Sullivan, who had ministered like angels to her every need, followed her with tears to the boat. Bishop Crimont was on board, and her great friend Captain John O'Brien, the king and darling of the northern seas, greeted her as "the riches of the ship."

In spite of all that all could do, and all vied generously in doing it, Mother Amadeus was very ill. It seemed more like a funeral procession than a trip. The nuns at Akulurak, not knowing her condition, had written that they must see her, and no word of ours could dissuade her from going. She had never given herself a thought; her body had ever been docile to her will's behest. There was some hope that the joy of going would be a benefit, even physical, the more so as there was a new mission to be founded. The Sisters of Providence were leaving Nome, and the Bishop wanted the Ursulines at Mary's Igloo ninety miles north of there.

The passage was a stormy one, but every day that the Bishop was able to be up, he came into the nuns' cabin and together we recited the Office of the Blessed Virgin. It was very touching and beautiful. The two great Alaskans had so long been friends, and the Queen of Alaska, "Our Lady of the Snows," looked lovingly down upon them as they prayed on the stormy sea.

One morning, Mother Amadeus awoke, feeling so much better, she said she was cured, and wanted to rise. I have no doubt now that God had worked the miracle, but then, I was afraid. I was afraid of the stormy sea, so wild and fierce. So I, unworthy, answered: "Oh, Mother let me go and call the Bishop." I went, and His Lordship told Mother Amadeus not to rise. A few nights later, the tumultuous sea threw her out of her berth. Helpless she lay, and we, with difficulty, got her back into the berth. We begged her to remain on board the *Victoria,* to return with it to Valdez where she could have more care, more comfort than at St. Michael, above all, where she could have milk, as milk was her only nourishment. But God's mysterious designs must be accomplished. Mother's face was set steadfastly to Akulurak as was Our Lord's to Jerusalem. She determined rather to spend a week at the hospital of St. Michael.

St. Ignatius day dawned. Mother Amadeus sent word to the Bishop that she could not wait another day for Holy Communion. The trip had been too stormy, the Bishop had been too ill to say Mass. Moreover his cabin was so small and poor that it would not admit of our entering. But after he had finished his Mass, kind Bishop Crimont brought the ciborium into Mother Amadeus' cabin. Thus did rays of celestial sunshine pierce the clouds of her declining years, and the Most Blessed Sacrament follow her with unchanging and ineffable tenderness.

On August 1st, the *Victoria* landed at St. Michael, and the commanding officer came on board to greet Mother Amadeus and to offer her the freedom of the Government hospital. There she remained a few days, receiving every available care, and the daily morning visit of Our Lord in Holy Communion. The *St. Joseph* was in port; Father Treca, too, presiding at the loading of the Mission boat and checking off the freight brought in by the *Victoria*. All St. Michael came to the holy bedside, and Mother Amadeus continued her apostolate comforting, directing, chiding the children who had erred. Her mind, her heart were absolutely unchanged and youthful, and she ruled like a queen from her sickbed.

And with the *St. Joseph* went Mother Amadeus of the Heart of Jesus to see her dear ones at Akulurak. We will let her tell the story of this trip.

Jesus!

December   KAHLEKAT IV   1919

Ursuline Convent, 2745 Mt. St. Helen's Place, Seattle, Wash.

No. 4

CHRONICLE OF THE NORTHLAND.

DEAR FRIEND:

You have read the story of the great, the magnetic Archbishop Seghers! It was in 1886 that he made his fourth, his last voyage to Alaska and there won the martyr's crown. In his heroism was Alaskan Mission life born. Two Jesuits, Fathers Tosi and Robaut, had gone with him, and in 1887 the Sisters of St. Ann followed to Holy Cross, Nulato and Dawson, whilst in 1905 went the Ursulines to St. Mary's the little Mission of which Kahlekat II. has told you. Then came our houses of St. Michael, Valdez, Mary's Igloo and Seattle, for the Alaskan Missionaries must have a trysting place in a milder climate where they may recover, every ten years or so, the strength worn by loneliness, cold and privation. In all these houses Our Lady sits enthroned, the Queen and Mistress, the first Superior, in favored shrines:

Our Lady of the Snow (St. Mary's)

Our Lady of the Propagation of the Faith (St. Michael's).

Our Lady of Peace (Valdez).

Our Lady of Peace and Plenty, (Seattle), and, lastly,

Mary's Igloo, Our Lady of Lourdes, on the Kruzgamipa River.

And beneath our altars lie the names of our benefactors, and before them do nuns and children kneel each day in grateful prayer. Yes, and the prayer of gratitude is always heard.

In July, 1918, I received an urgent call from my nuns in the North, and I sailed on the boat that carried the Rt. Rev. R. J. Crimont, S. J., first Bishop of Alaska. The *Victoria* and the great King and Darling of the Northern Seas, Captain John O'Brien, brought us to St. Michael on August 1st. There at St. Ursula's-by-the-Sea, were we greeted by two of the oldest Alaskan Missionaries of the Jesuit Order, Father Robaut and Father Treca. It was like plunging into the heart of the past to talk with these two missionaries and the great Jesuit Bishop. But our time was limited, and soon the *St. Joseph* broke from its moorings to carry us to Akulurak. The Bishop and Father Treca came, too. Medieval it was and most sweet to float leisurely down the St. Michael Canal in company so holy, past Cape Romanoff out to sea, then into the Aphoon, the North mouth of the Yukon Delta, to Old Hamilton, down the Apenkar to the Akulurak and St. Mary's, stopping at night that the crew might rest, or whenever a duck attracted the aim of our sailor boys, or to let down the lifeboat when some missionary labor called to the heart of the priest: some child to baptize, some marriage to bless or sanctify, some traveler hence to anoint, some little child calling from the villages on the shore that it wished to go to the Mission school. We were not in a hurry. Little recked we the white settlements as our convent floated down the great river.

On the feast of the Assumption, very early, our little craft stopped at the landing, and the Mission dogs awakened all by the lusty call that the *St. Joseph* had arrived. The gangplank was thrown down and then came the joyous meeting with nuns and children. After an early Mass on the *St. Joseph* we assisted in the Mission church at the Pontifical Mass at which our Bishop was assisted by Revs. Lucchesi and Treca as Deacon and Sub-Deacon, the children singing in faultless Plain Chant at the feet of "Our Lady of the Snows."

A too short visit, and off went the *St. Joseph* into winter quarters at Holy Cross.

But as we swept adown the glorious river, past Andreaffsky, where the delta begins, the sight of trees, the willow alder, cottonwood, low fir, hemlock, and birch began to gladden our vision and the many summer fishing camps of our people, with their nets and weirs and fishing wheels, their racks where the salmon hang to dry in the sun. It was worthy of the apostolic days to see the *St. Joseph* stop to gather children for the Mission school, as the cry came from the shore that some poor waif asked the protection of Mother Church. It was Judea and Our Lord come back to let down our Bishop to meet the resident missionary and his people, and follow them in his august humility to the church to administer the Sacrament of Confirmation. Oh! the benignity of the purple, the awful familiarity of the Eskimos toward this, the first granted them by Rome!

How far are we now from Archbishop Seghers, the martyr of Alaska? How far from Peter, the Prince of Bishops? And could there be a fitter setting for the great Sacrament than the nearness of the very poor in their unwavering, unquestioning faith? For the Spirit breathes upon the lowly. The foolish grandeur of earth is too immeasurably removed. Happy, happy, the exchange! And after the ceremony, our dear people would crowd on to the little *St. Joseph* to receive from the nuns some memento of the great day, and to see the boat off with shouts and greetings. At Holy Cross we awaited the river steamer *Sarah,* and hastened down the river again to St. Michael. We were accompanied this time by the Honorable Thomas Riggs, Governor of Alaska, the first builder of the railroad, of the Alaska boundary line, and the lovely Mrs. Riggs, a fervent, distinguished Catholic lady, both laboring nobly and generously for the welfare of the poor Eskimo people.

Again our stay at St. Ursula's-by-the-Sea was too short. I wrote you how, on December 9th, it became the prey of flames. We were not settled down to our long winter rest, when the dreadful visitation of the influenza rudely awakened us. It fastened its deadly grip on the Eskimos, and the Yukon became a charnel house. The people were sick, starving, for a cruel quarantine cut them off from St. Michael from December 3d to February 10th. Not even the dogs were allowed to run lest they should carry the germs of infection. Our poor people died in great numbers, especially the young mothers, many of them wandering out of their cabins to die in the snow when the hand of charity was stretched out to rescue them. Our noble Governor and Mrs. Riggs organized relief parties and the Fathers traveled back and forth, carrying ice and wood to the hovels that the people might not die, and bringing medicine for both soul and body. But even this dark hour was God's hour. The children flocked in numbers to the Mission, where they will drink in Catholicity from the cradle, free from the superstition every Eskimo baby sucks with the mother milk. And so the sad winter wore on. Nuns and children, by God's mercy, were spared, and the summer came again. The birds began to "tsip! tsip!" long before the mercury rose or the ice went out, and we listened, enchanted, to the gurgle of running water. This seems the sweetest of all earthly music to the ear weary of the long silence of ice and snow. You wonder at first what the joyous whisper of Nature is, and then suddenly you know,—you know that the second chapter of the Alaskan year, the thaw, is at hand. It is inebriating with delight. The birds come north in uncounted millions and the sweet chirp of the white crowned sparrow, the Alaskan nightingale, begins to pour gladness into the lengthening day and into the heart of the Northlander. The ptarmigan that has spent the winter with us in robes of snowy white, streaks itself in brown as the tundra peeps up from beneath the snow and furrows the sides of the stately Mt. St. Michael. Then do we turn our eyes skyward and wager for the coming of the first goose. Its clanging seems to us the burst of martial music, and all St. Michael is out of doors. "The goose! The goose!" as children follow the band about our city streets. For the goose is the unpaid, the unerring weather prophet. She cannot be mistaken. She is heaven's "first boat," and oh! Alaskans know what the "first boat" means. How welcome the revenue cutter *Bear*, the dauntless *Victoria!* How gracefully, how gratefully they dip and ride the opening water! Yes, all St. Michael looks at the goose, rubbing its eyes as one who awakens from a long, hard dream. Behold the auklets on the cliffs; the smile of the barren rocks, the ptarmigan clad in brown, the swans. The cranes circle high in air, the curlew lifts its long legs, the phalarope swings back and forth on its own strangely busy business, and the ducks attract the unerring aim of the Eskimos. As are the dogs in winter, so are the birds in summer, our great delight. Our life is marked by two epochs; the freeze up with the dogs, the thaw with the migratory birds. Nor spring, nor fall comes to us. The mountains of snow are suddenly swallowed up by the thousand mouths of the porous soil, and we begin to listen for the first whistle of the boats.

And now, what flowers have grown for the Lord in this garden of Northern planting? Are there any lilies here? What, here? Where ice and snow rule for eight months of the year and the birds' faint chirp is heard only in the short moist summer? Yes, the ashes of Archbishop Seghers have been fruitful.

First there was the angelic child "Noonaki" whom we called the "Little Flower" of our Arctic field. She had an uplifting smile for all. Her example, in its sinlessness, was inspiration. For four years she lay stretched out on a bed of suffering in patience, unruffled by pain, uncertainty, weariness. A living pulpit was Noonaki, where even the commanding officer of Fort St. Michael and others went to hear the lovely sermon of Catholic maidenhood. She died early on April 29th, after having long been a weekly, nay, a daily communicant. God lifted up this little girl of Eskimo birth, "from the dung-hill to a place among the princes of His people."

She left behind her mourning "Sagnak," her school girl friend. This child of ours—and no Ursuline child could be a prouder boast—is directress of the choir and lets her sweet, rich voice ring out as she plays, and the ladies of the Post follow her baton at Christmas and Easter. Prudent, maidenly, womanly, is Sagnak. She rules her mother's household in spotless cleanliness, while she holds high the beacon light of good example in Innuit land. How proud she is of her brother Saggak! Saggak is the only native Alaskan that crossed the seas and met the enemy in open battle. Think of it. This is what he writes his sister from "Somewhere in France"—his uncorrected letter:

"Was at the front in Belgium twice in nine days at the France front, and I was hite by high explosive shell through my gas mask, but stop outside of my coat, and I was very luck not got hurt, and (censored) or (boys censored) were hurt all around me, and my Corp? was hurt and the boy lay alongside of me he lost his right am. We certainly had very hard time of it not much sleep and cold rain nights, and all the big artillery shell fires and machine gun fires flying all over us. And marching days and nights we do certainly have some war experience at the front line in France and Belgium. When we was at Belgium front line artillery shell fires I was cooking flap jack out of Belgium flour which it has been left in the house and sour milk, I mix it up and started to cook it and it was three of us in the house. And the German start shelling us before we get through, and when big high explosive shell strike to the house and broke all the windows down and I ran down to the basement and I stay down there for while, and we lost our first officer there and 4 other men and our flap jacks, and I am now very glad that great war is over.

"I expect to go home sometime I have a proud place to fill and you know now I will do this honorably and bravely. The weather it is now we have just fine, the country looks fine but lonesome place. The French people cannot understand English. Just a few days ago I took some washing to French woman and ask her if she can wash my clothes and she said something in French, but I did not understand what she said, but I make a signs with my hands 'wash' and also she make a signs 'bring it.' And last night I went over there her house and stand front of her and I give her good big smile, and she give my laundry."

We must not forget our dear "Bunyak" the fairy worker in fur and wampum. She has adopted a beautiful little white boy, one of those waifs to whom even an Eskimo name and home are an honor, a protection. And how clean, how holy, is the Christian, Catholic home of Bunyak and Joseph. More than once have I entrusted to her errands that required zeal and discretion, and she has acquitted herself of them faultlessly. "Ekoonak," too, is an honor as she sings in the choir, Sagnak's chief support, or accompanies Henry on his yearly hunts for fur and seal.

Our children's households are thoroughly Catholic, civilized. It is a joy to see the full fruition of the promise they gave the love with which we encompassed their youth.

Have the missionaries been idle? Have your dear alms lain fallow? Was the noble blood of Archbishop Seghers shed in vain?

And now one word more Kahlekat IV. would whisper. she is a beggar with a wallet on her arm. Drop your alms, great or small, that she may live till her Sister comes, Kahlekat V., on another Christmas day to keep her wooden wedding. The days, the hours, are anxious, but

> Behind the dim unknown
> Standeth God within the shadow
> Keeping watch above His own.

Seven of ours sailed north on July 30th—two for the old, and five for the new mission at Mary's Igloo, "Our Lady of Lourdes"—where they will protect and save the little Catholic orphans, given us by the influenza. Their letters are bubbling over with unselfish joy, unconscious heroism. Oh! where are the strong young arms willing to labor with us in the field white for the harvest? Alms we need, yes, but workers, too, for we that have digged the furrows are grown old, and we call to you, beautiful young generation, as did the gladiators of old: *"Morituri salutamus."* You know the harships, you know not the joys of the life, the super-abounding sweetness of Christ Our Lord at the close of one of those days of absolute self-surrender. There is an almost divine simplicity in the souls of the children which is a joy. And, oh! there are those secrets whispered at Holy Communion which fill the solitude with the music of love. Little dreams the world of love in its wildest vagaries, for true love leans its heart against the door of the Tabernacle, where dwells the Maker, the King of Love. Come ye workers, buoyant in the perennial strength of the super-natural. Other lives, too, are full of the supernatural, but the supernatural in disguise, trammeled by the petty comforts, the exigencies, the reticences, the restrictions of civilization and surroundings, the requirements of higher edu-

cation in its curriculum, its rush, its competition with the
world. In Alaska, the supernatural is free, untrammeled,
naked as it were, crying out from night till morning, ar
from morning till night. This is the secret that Kal at
IV. had to tell, and now it leaves you with one last word
and that is from the Prophet Isaias:

"Deal thy bread to the hungry, and bring the needy and
harborless into thy house; when thou shalt see one naked,
cover him, and despise not thy own flesh. Then shall thy
light break forth as the morning, and thy health shall
speedily arise, and thy justice shall go before thy face, and
the glory of the Lord shall gather thee up. Then shalt thou
call, and the Lord shall hear; thou shalt cry and He shall
say, Here I am."

Merry Christmas, dear friend. Drop you alms into Kahlekat's wallet for the love of the dear Christ Child of Beth-
lehem.

I have told you all, "Nish," as our Indians say, drawing
the palm of one hand up against the other, "I have finished."

Your unforgetting friend,

SISTER MARY AMADEUS OF THE HEART OF JESUS,
Superior of the Ursulines of Alaska.

CHAPTER XXII

The Shadows of Death Close In About Her

Our world shall it turn colder
   Now cold suns wane?
Draw closer growing older!
   Our hearts shall gain
From dearer love a warmer glow
Than in the golden song-time long ago!

O, snow-time has its joyance
   Its buds of hope;
Love reaches then claivoyance,
   And sunsets ope
Gateways to visions more sublime
Than any sunrise of the summer's prime!

The end near? Wherefore sadness to know it, dear?
   At winter's end comes gladness,
The new spring's cheer!
Love in the frost can feel no threat—
The earth remembers; can the heart forget?[1]

IN spite of weakness and great fatigue, Mother Amadeus visited the nuns at Akulurak and spread the sweet odor of her virtues at the wonderful Mission of Holy Cross. Here the Sisters of St. Anne had received her with exquisite loveliness and hospitality. Founded many years before ours, on the banks of the Yukon, their Mission had long attracted the wondering glances of all travelers to the North. There is no book that does not mention Holy Cross, the show place of all Alaska.

[1] *At Winter's End*, by Stokely S. Fisher. Words copied by our dear Mother for her life-long companion, and found after her holy death.

Miss Robins, in her *Magnetic North*, has placed there some of her sweetest scenes. But Mother Amadeus had never before had the opportunity to visit it.

Upon her return to St. Michael she settled down with unspeakable joy in the sweetest home we had ever known, St. Ursula's-by-the-Sea. The home so tiny, was hung with memories of the dear benefactors who had made it habitable. A rich library had been contributed to this our distributing point for Alaska, and our people had made for us a museum, artistic along Eskimo lines. The chapel, decorated by the munificence of Mrs. Ryan and others, was so beautiful the Bishop called it "My Little Cathedral." The altar nestled in an alcove built for it, and upon the Thabor sparkled on Exposition days, the Ostensorium, sent by the Ursulines of Cleveland, before which the little Sarah Theresa Dunne used to pray in her childhood days. The nave was large enough, the parlor doors being thrown open, to accommodate St. Michael's congregation during the winter months. And our precious invalid, now in her chair, now from her bed, kept her eyes riveted upon the Blessed Sacrament. She seemed to improve in the busy peace of "Home Sweet Home," whatever blasts might blow, for the Eskimos crowded about her as their queen, and the white settlers, especially Mrs. Franklin Moses, paid her the homage of kindness and respect.

On the feast of St. Jude, October 28th, however, Mother Amadeus fell from her chair. Our prayers for her cure had been unusually fervent that day, and we hoped that the "Saint of the Impossible" would cure her. Left alone an instant, she leaned for support on a chair. It gave way. We found her stretched in great pain on the floor. It was the first sound of the death knell, ringing clear and sharp from heaven. Gently we lifted her into her bed, and called our good friend Dr. Love—the eminent physician at Fort St. Michael. Mother Amadeus never walked again, and the doctor whispered to her nurse as he left her room: "Sister, it is the beginning of the end. You must take Mother to Seattle by the last boat that leaves in a few days."

But the great apostle wanted to die at her post, and we yielded to the saintliness and strength of her will. She grew more joyous, more energetic, planning, working from her bed, talking about the new Mission she had come north to open on the Kruzgamipa River ninety miles north of Nome. Trunks were filled with things her wonderful memory recalled in the upper rooms she had not seen in years, and we were happy in spite of the shadow looming dark and ominous.

On the evening of December 5th, Father Robaut came over, as usual, to hear our confessions. I noticed an unwonted light in our Mother's eyes, something like the twinkle of a child who knows a secret. But my great reverence for her silenced the question that kept rising to my lips. The next morning, after Mother Amadeus had received Holy Communion and had taken her breakfast, she said to me with a smile and the old ringing laugh of the long ago: "Sister, prepare the room, and when it is ready, call Father Robaut. He has promised to anoint me today."

Death was in my heart, joy in hers! All the flowers we had—artificial ones of course, sent by our benefactors—were placed about, and many candles lighted in the little cell. The life of St. Angela in pictures we hung about the bed, and Carpaccio's St. Ursula, and when I thought all was ready, Mother Amadeus said: "Place over me the beautiful lace Mrs. Ryan gave me, and lay upon the Altar the pall Mother Blessed Sacrament embroidered for my Golden Jubilee." She looked like a bride. She was joyous, buoyant and exceedingly beautiful. It seemed more like a First Communion day than a room prepared for Extreme Unction. "Now, Sister, call Father Robaut." He came, the first Jesuit to set his foot in Alaska, the companion of the martyr Archbishop Seghers. and with him came also the Very Rev. J. B. Sifton, Superior of the Jesuits in Northern Alaska. And the most beautiful rite of the Church unfolded before us. *"Per istam sanctum unctionem!"* She answered every prayer, followed with exuberant joy every move, so that when he came to anoint her pure eyes, Father Robaut was obliged to whisper. "Close your eyes." Ah! the saints, the saints! Why should they not be winning who live in perpetual union with Our Lord? And from that day forward, the shadow of things human rested not upon Mother Amadeus of the Heart of Jesus. She bade farewell to earth, and thought only of heaven.

The feast of the Immaculate Conception fell on Sunday. It had always been a day of special grace for Mother Amadeus. Masses were celebrated in our chapel as the Church could not be heated because of the intense cold. Many of our people came to Holy Communion, and Mother Amadeus had breakfast served them in our tiny kitchen. Among them came, toward the end, a poor erring one who had strayed far from the Banquet of the Angels. She rushed in saying: I must see Father." Long was her confession, then she, too, tasted of the sweetness of the King.

Our people have many of the instincts of child-hood and of nature. Something special attracted them to our Mother and to the Convent on that day. The door of her room faced the altar; it had been thrown open, and she had assisted at Mass from her bed. At benediction the children had sung all her favorite hymns, and our boy Francis had accompanied them on his violin. Before leaving, all crowded about her bed. Each must have some word, some special sign of recognition.

And when all was over, the huge snow drifts locked our doors and cloistered us with our happiness, with Our Lord in the sweetest solitude we had ever known. No one came. No one could come that day. We were so happy together. It seems, in the retrospect, that we might have guessed it was our last day at St. Ursula's-by-the-Sea. The next morning early we were affrighted by dense clouds of smoke. We had but time to lift our precious invalid out into the 40° below zero and to call the Father to save the Most Blessed Sacrament.

In twenty minutes St. Ursula's-by-the-Sea was a heap of ashes, for there is no water in Northern Alaska eight months of the year, and snow and ice are of no avail in case of fire. All our treasures went. Our Lord was telling His Spouse that He was henceforth her sole possession. We hurried her into shelter, and sent for Dr. Love. Mother Amadeus was bearing up bravely. When he came she said to him in her own dear way, "Well, Doctor, the Lord gave; the Lord hath taken away. Blessed be the name of the Lord!"

So bright, so wonderful was she that again hope began to sing a sweet song in our ears. Not so to wise Dr. Love. "The reaction will soon set in," he whis-

MOTHER AND KOKOMIKIS.

pered. "Do not fail to send for me." And it did set in with fearful violence. Exposure had brought the most excruciating rheumatic pains in the injured hip, and these scarcely abated during the five months that she still remained at St. Michael. It was crucifixion. Indeed, hard nails driven into the hip could not have caused keener suffering. Mother Amadeus kept exclaiming, her eyes lifted up to Heaven, "May the most high, the most holy, the most just will of God be done! May it be forever praised and glorified." Captain Cummings, U. S. A. Commanding Officer of Fort St. Michael, with unspeakable goodness and generosity, offered her the hospitality of one of the officers' quarters left vacant. There we moved and the Most Blessed Sacrament came too, and we had our chapel and continued teaching all who could come to us. Every morning Mother Amadeus received Holy Communion whatever had been her tortures of the night, and during the day, when pain abated, Captain Cummings, his wife, his lovely little girls, the officers, the soldiers, the Eskimos, came to sun themselves in her saintly presence.

One of the soldiers, W. A. Kelley, was preparing for baptism. In and out of the sick room he would glide, "in his port as meek as a maid," keeping up the fire, bringing coal and helping the nurse when her strength did not suffice. And all this so gently and so kindly that Mother called him "Sister William." He made his First Communion in our chapel, and came every Sunday morning to Mass, Confession and Holy Communion there. So that though we had lost everything, a tender Providence still watched over us even in that dark, sad hour.

Our people often found their way into Mother

Amadeus' room, and silent and tearful, with the true delicacy of the heart, they would steal away when they saw signs of pain on the face they loved so well. Sagnak weeping said: "Mother reminds me of the Blessed Virgin."

On the last feast of the Ascension she celebrated on earth, the kind Father, fearing she would die at sea, had anointed her for the second time, for the first boat was to take Mother Amadeus to Seattle.

Meanwhile, St. Ursula's-by-the-Sea was rebuilding, and the birds were coming north and the snow was vanishing. Mother Amadeus has herself written the poetry of the returning spring to Alaska in Kahlekt IV., the rough draft of which she alone saw. Her heart was full of gentleness and of love. The war had come, the armistice had come, and never a word on the subject had crossed her lips. The victim of love knew only words of love. At length the *Victoria* came. Snow was still on the smmmits, the ice was floating on the sea. The officials of the Navigation Company provided gentle means, and Mother Amadeus was safely carried on to the *Meteor*, and lifted, by crane and derrick, in what we Alaskans call the "Cage" from the little boat safe on to the deck of the big one. All St. Michael crowded on the *Victoria* to see her off, and many a prayer was breathed for the safety of the boat with its prize. She seemed to grow a little better, and could bear to be lifted from her berth into an easy chair in the cabin. And she used to sit there for hours looking at the ocean she had always loved so well. God "tempered the wind" once more to the shorn lamb. By His gentle mercy, the sea was placid as a lake all the way. She enjoyed greeting, from a distance, the two boats so famous in Alaskan waters, *The Bear* and *The Polar Bear*.

Tortured as her body was, her soul was full of peace and joy. She gathered up sufficient strength to give her last directions to her companion, to express her most sacred wish, to give to her beloved benefactors her thanks, her greetings, her promise of prayer for them before the throne of God. Then she fell into the mysterious silence of Gethsemane. Not the silence of impotence, but the silence of sovereign will, plighted this many a year to penance and sacrifice. She began her immediate preparation for death. Christ, the Lord, she knew, was very near.

Upon reaching the convent in Seattle she said: "It is like Heaven here with my dear nuns about me." Again, when the missionaries started off for the new Mission, "Our Lady of Lourdes," on Kruzgamipa River, she gave them her last blessing, and turning to her companion said: "What a pity that you and I cannot go with them." Bishop Crimont, Bishop O'Dea, many of her Jesuit friends, all Seattle's Sisterhoods, came to her bedside, and countless friends.

Twice she received the blessing of our late Holy Father, Pope Benedict XV. The first came on the eve of the Assumption, telegraphed direct from the Vatican:

Roma, 1919, Aug. 14, 2 P. M.
"Pregando alla inferma Madra Amadea aiuti e comforti celesti, Augusto Pontefice le accorda, con paterno affetto, implorata benedizione Apostolica.
"CARDINAL GASPARRI."

A second pontifical blessing came before the end, the blessing too of Cardinal Guistini, the Ursuline Protector, and loving greetings from the Mother General.

The victim of love smiling constantly with great joy, followed with her eyes those who came and went, sometimes speaking to her kind physician, Dr. W. J. Griffith, who saw her every day. It was generally to tell him that she was very happy, and he would smile and go away with tears in his big, kind heart. Though two of the nuns slept in Mother Amadeus' room every night, she never disturbed them. They would find her lying there, her eyes wide open, smiling at the darkness, her lips moving in prayer, but they had learned to guess her needs. Toward morning she would fall asleep, but love always awakened her in time for Mass and Holy Communion. Her bed had been moved into the parlor which was contiguous to the chapel, so that she lived her last months in Seattle, as she had lived at St. Michael, in the uninterrupted presence of her great, her only love, the Most Blessed Sacrament.

On July 10th she was anointed for the third time, and again on the First Friday, November 7th. That afternoon the Rt. Rev. E. J. O'Dea, Bishop of Seattle, gave her his last last blessing, and lingered long at her bedside. On the nights of the 8th and of the 9th, three nuns watched her with inexpressible anxiety; they could see her slipping away from them, do what they might. On the morning of the 10th, Mother Amadeus received Holy Communion and heard Mass as usual. But her breathing was labored ,and in the chapel could be heard the constant whisper: "My Jesus, mercy!"

After Mass, Mother Dosithée came up to Mother and said, "Kiss me happy feast, Mother, it is the anniversary of my profession." She responded with the angelic smile of Motherhood. Then she tried to swallow a few drops of milk, but could not, and we gathered about her knowing that the end was now at hand. Her eyes dropped, and deflected toward the Tabernacle and her lips kept framing the words: "My Jesus, mercy." Rev. Father Vasta, S. J., and Father McGrath, our assistant pastor, Dr. Griffin, said the prayers for the agonizing and ministered to her. At just exactly 11:15 on the morning of November 10, 1919, she looked up and smiled, a smile of triumph and joy and recognition. Something beautiful and beloved Mother Amadeus saw in that last supreme moment. Then she closed her eyes, and all was over. Pain had fled; the battle was won.

CHAPTER XXIII

LAYING HER TO REST

THE nuns lifted their Mother's lifeless form reverently onto a cross of ashes, and then intoned the *"De Profundis"* and, as she had magnanimously taught them in hours of sorrow, the *"Te Deum."* The sacred corpse was then prepared for burial. It was embalmed, then placed in a copper coffin hermetically sealed. That was laid in a vault of concrete weighing very close on to a ton and conveyed to St. Ignatius Mission for burial. Three nuns accompanied it and at Ravalli Station, Ursulines and Jesuits met the relics. The long sad line filed over the hills to St. Ignatius Mission, and placed Mother Amadeus once more in the chapel she loved so well, that she herself founded thirty years before. Nuns watched all night in prayer, and gazed upon the loved countenance to which death had given back all its youth, all its beauty. They took her blessed hands in theirs, and noticed that the prayers they said to her were granted. Those hands had ever had the "King's gift." They had always soothed and comforted! Those who had never seen Mother Amadeus in life exclaimed when they saw her thus: "Oh! how beautiful."

The next day the children and the Indians crowded in to behold her. One old squaw took from her head a black silk handkerchief, and fumbling in the corner showed the nuns the letters in red marking cotton, S. M. A., Mother Amadeus' mark. "One day," she said, when Mother was in the sled, ready to leave the Mis-

216

sion, I came to tell her good-bye. She took this handkerchief that the nuns had just tied around her neck—
it was very cold—and she tied it around my head. I
wear it only on great occasions." Then she cried and
sobbed, old Katrina, the model of the Flathead women.

The morning of November 13th broke dark and
cloudy. The Very Rev. Father Rockliffe, S. J., so long
and so greatly beloved as Superior and Provincial, in
his Order, said Mass in the convent chapel. At eight
thirty six stalwart Flatheads (one of them boasted that
he had driven Mother Amadeus over from Ravalli when
she had come in 1890 to found the Mission, and had
been the first to give his child to the Kindergarten),
Lomais, Trout, Frank, Joseph, Peter, Choute, lifted the
sacred remains and carried them into the great Mission
Church. They laid them beneath the frescoed painting of St. Angela receiving from St. Ursula the banner
of the Order.

Father Bruckert offered the High Mass of Requiem,
assisted by Fathers Post and Buddy as Deacon and Sub-
deacon. The Sisters and children sang the Requiem
Mass. After the Mass Very Rev. Father Rockliffe stood
beside the holy corpse and spoke of the sadness of
death from the natural point of view; of the glory and
triumph of death from the supernatural point of view
for one who had striven to follow Our Lord as closely,
as lovingly as Mother Amadeus had. And Father Post
spoke of the dear dead to the Indians in the Flathead
language.

Then the chief men among the Flatheads lifted the
sacred remains again. And as they did so, the tribe
burst forth in its dirge for the departed heroes of the
race. She was one of them. No human word can ren-

der the pathos and grandeur of this song. It rises and
falls in quarter tones. To an accompaniment of base
voices like the wailing of the mountain winds in winter, rises to the highest human pitch, a female voice
that sobs. At one point the shrill notes seem to cry:
"Come back! Come back!" in the anguish of despair,
and then the voice slides imperceptibly down again,
until it is lost once more in the soughing of the basic
harmonies. These children of the Rockies have caught
from Nature the secret of understanding grief and
soothing it. Not Beethoven, not Chopin, not Mendels-
sohn, has written a more heart-searching funeral
march. It was caught up by the winds of St. Mary's
Lake, and moaned, again and again, in the echoes of
the great Rocky Mountains.

It took an hour to reach the God's Acre in a
secluded spot just at the foot of the Main Range. Here
rest too, the other sacred remains, the nuns, the Jesuits;
Fathers Menentray, Van Gorp Dela Mott, D'Aste, Mu-
set and others, wonderful missionaries all of them,
Pablo and the great men of the Flathead tribe.

As the sacred remains were lowered into the vault,
the sun, which up to that time had been hidden under
dark clouds, burst out into a golden smile, the smile
of the Father bidding His child welcome home. A
granite cross, planted in a rock, marks the spot and
says to the passer-by: "Here rests, awaiting the resurrection, the mortal part of the Rev. Mother Amadeus
of the Heart of Jesus, Foundress of the Ursuline Missions of Montana and Alaska, who died at the Ursuline
Convent of Seattle, November 10, 1919, R. I. P. Our
Lady of the Blessed Sacrament pray for us."

"Si monumentum quæris, circumspice."

CHAPTER XXIV

Rev. Mother Amadeus of the Heart of Jesus As Her Nuns Saw Her

"And I have felt a Presence that disturbs me
With the joy of elevated thoughts."—*Wordsworth*.

"The beautiful external part of sanctity is that it transforms the large and deep qualities of natural character. It does not destroy; it fulfills."

Time wipes away, in its merciless advance, the memory of ordinary men and women. Not so the glory of God's special friends. Mother Amadeus of the Heart of Jesus is one of those whose name will live, not only in the hearts of her many spiritual children, but also in a wider sphere. She was an organizer, a pioneer, and she has stamped her name upon the soil of Montana and Alaska. "The Mother" she was called by Whites, Indians, and Eskimos. No other name describes her so well or so well satisfies her children's admiring love. I was one of them. Love impels me to lift the curtain and show her as we knew her.

At the first General Chapter of our Old Order, November, 1900, the Spiritual Director who met so many for the first time, singled Mother Amadeus out as one preëminently supernatural.

She waited always for God's direction in things great and small. She was but the tool which the Master hand raised or let drop as He would. Sometimes people said that she was slow. Yet whilst she waited, she labored

with untiring energy, unconquerable firmness, and
when once she had begun, she was prompt, irresistible,
ready. She never turned back, seldom changed her
mind. Her success in our work lay in her choice of
subjects for the various employments.

Simple as the Shepherd's, royal and energetic as the
Magi's was her faith, firm, buoyant, perennially youthful like St. Theresa's. From faith, proceeded firmness,
and great indifference to the opinions, the criticisms of
men. Her eyes, her heart were fixed upon God; hence
strong was her arm, prompt and unswerving her action.

Holy Communion, the Rule, Regular Observance ab-
sorbed her capacity for belief. She did not seek the ex-
traordinary, but was content to see "darkly as in a glass"
now, but then "face to face." The Catholic instincts given
by her parents struck deep roots. Later this faith shone
forth in all its radiance! When, in 1900 and 1906, she
was presented to Popes Leo XIII., and Pius X., both
Pontiffs, though so different, singled Mother out for
marks of special benevolence, and on March 2, 1906,
when she called at the Lateran to see our Protector,
"Mother Amadeus," he exclaimed on beholding that
countenance for the first time, "have you a heart of
gold?"

At the Chapter Mother Amadeus held at St. Peter's
when Cardinal Vannutelli's letter came proposing the
terms and conditions of Canonical Union, she told us
that the Pope's slightest wish was an order, and so
strong was her faith, so magnetic, we felt that, though
open in form, the Union was closed in fact to heart and
conscience.

When she started for Rome with her secretary and
a little Flathead girl, she had not heard of anyone else

going, but she had Bishop Brondel's approval; nothing could stop her.

Faith, I may say, was resplendent in every act of her great life. Was it not faith that led her without certain means of support out into Montana at the word of Bishop Gilmour, "God never sends a bird into the forest without providing for it, my child." Again we see her breaking away from her first foundation in Miles City, and going at the call of Bishop Brondel and Father Damiani into the mountain wilderness of St. Peter's with only two novices and two postulants. And when illness brought her to death's door on the floor of the poor log cabin, she commended the four young souls with unruffled faith to God's keeping.

That seed of faith blossomed into abundant fruit, not only in Montana, but also in Alaska and in the Canonical Union. How fearlessly, leaning upon the rod of faith, she went to Rome! How unselfishly she fell back into the ranks when the Union was voted November 21, 1900.

Companion of faith, hope shone forth in all her actions. She loved the little Saint of Hope, the "Little Flower of Jesus." When in 1896, at the beck of A. P.A.ism, Congress withdrew our appropriation, Mother Amadeus' trust in Providence kept our Missions open. We had then one thousand Indian girls under our care.

Once, in going through the well-filled store-rooms of the great Georgetown Visitation Convent in 1893, Mother was much struck by a little card framed and hung upon the wall: the promise of Our Lord to St. Margaret Mary: "Remember thou shalt want succor only when I want power." The nuns, seeing her eyes rest lovingly upon the little card, detached it and gave it to her. Mother brought this token lovingly back with her to St. Peter's, hung it beside her poor little six feet by twenty-five inch bed, and made it the subject of her joyful meditations during many a long and sleepless night. Despite lack of money and scarcity of subjects she went right on. "God commands the work," she thought, "He will provide the means." Her unswerving, buoyant trust, was catching and peculiarly characteristic. Yet she was as active, intelligent, and prudent, as untiring in her work as though its success depended entirely on herself, and upon herself alone.

To speak of Mother Amadeus' charity is to rewrite her life, so utterly does charity pervade and permeate it.

Beginning with God, descending through the Blessed Virgin, St. Joseph, the angels, and saints, especially the great and little Theresa of Carmel, the patrons of our Order, her love nestled in the hearts of her spiritual children, her family, friends, and benefactors, till it reached, with undiminished intensity, the waifs of the Indians and Eskimos. The glimpses of her home life that have come to us, in Toledo as postulant, novice, Superior, show us a magnetism over hearts unsurpassed if ever equaled.

Whenever she left us for her visits to the Missions, her last words were always: "Practice charity; be watchful over the children." Mother Amadeus longed intensely for the contemplative, enclosed life, as so many of our great Ursulines have and do, but her love for the waifs of humanity led her to sacrifice that longing. She rejoiced greatly at the arrival of each child, each postulant, each professed nun sent to offer help to the needy Missions. She never wearied, never rested when there was question of souls. For years she feared

death as many of the saints have done, and yet she
never hesitated to expose herself to danger in her quest
for souls. Magnanimously did the Arch-lover of souls
reward her, for when death came, fear dropped off like
a worn out mantle and she went to sleep peacefully in
His arms.

"Spend yourself for God. Throw away the body,"
she wrote during her annual retreats. Like the great
Theresa, Mother Amadeus could say, "Thank God, I have
been beloved wherever I have been. To give pleasure
to others, I always forgot myself even to excess." She
loved as did Our Lord, "unto the end." Treachery,
abandonment could not weary her. She never forgot
a birthday, a sacred anniversary of her parents, her
friends, her nuns, or their relatives. Her tenderness to
the sick was beyond all that the heart can express, her
diagnosis unerring, her expense lavish in spite of poverty.

She hung over her dear children whilst there was
breath in their bodies, and after their deaths she would
remain for days in grief so silent, so deep that we durst
not mention their names. I remember in particular
Agessa's death. Mother Amadeus was away, but we
recalled her and she arrived on the eve. When she
came up to the sick bed, the little Indian maiden, who
till then had not been able to hold up her head, sat up
in bed, and folded her arms about Mother, pressing her
to her heart as though she would have her penetrate it.
All night Mother watched the child and listened and
looked when Agessa said she saw Our Lord, clad in red
and bearing a heavy cross. Mother was in every sense
the friend. She could afford both to hear and speak the
truth. She never gave a compliment; yet she knew

how to lift up your heart in hours of discouragement. She never expressed her love in words, but ah! her actions! Her heart was an incandescent flame of love kindled by God in the dear Heart of Jesus. How hard it must have been for her to repress, as she did, every exterior mark of affection.

I have seen the most difficult characters grow tractable and lovable by contact with her. She had a mother's heart, and a mother's heart is the most perfect thing God has ever made. What was the source of her charm, her magnetism? Was it, as in Venerable Mary of the Incarnation, her unbroken union with God? I have never seen Mother, night or day, in sickness or comparative health, traveling or at home, oppressed with business or at recreation that she did not seem united to God. This same impression came to our first Mother General when first she beheld Mother Amadeus and the Very Rev. J. Lemius, O.M.I., Procurator General of the great Missionary Order, the Oblates of Mary Immaculate, said after his first glimpse, "Her chief trait is that she is so supernatural." Yet she was so gay, so simple, so ineffably kind. "Only by the lines of her mouth," said a Superior of one of our German houses, "did I discover her great firmness. The rest of her face is winning, irresistible charm and sweetness."

Mother Amadeus always preferred, for her sphere of action, the humble beginnings, the organization of houses. She loved the poverty of Montana and Alaska! I think one of the greatest sorrows of her life was to be elected Provincial of the North of the United States which cut her off from residence among the poor. The log cabin was dear to her above all, because there poverty was most vividly depicted. She lived in log cabins

at St. Peter's, in log cabins at St. Labre's, in log cabins
at St. Paul's, and in Alaska! dear Alaska! And she always left them with regret.

With a proud maternal smile she saw that other
great missionary, Sister Mary Magdalen, get supper in our log cabin kitchen with an umbrella fixed
over the stove, and wading herself cheerfully and
simply knee-deep in water. The poor roof was leak-
ing. She took it all simply as a matter of course.
Mother Amadeus bought nothing for herself. We had
to keep a sharp outlook on her personal needs. All
remember her beautiful penmanship, clear and legible
as print. She wrote constantly and yet she crucified
herself by the use of pen points long since grown worthless. We had to steal them away at last and replace
them by newer ones at the risk of a sorrowful glance
of reprehension. How very poor, cramped, anxious she always was in human things! How reposeful,
broad, lavish always in the divine. We lived on alms,
depended upon the daily mails for support, and the
many needs of the work. Hence poverty weighed heavily upon Mother's shoulders.

When we were in Rome for the first Chapter General
in 1900, Mother Amadeus took a carriage only when
circumstances obliged her to,—the lateness of the hour
—for we had to be in the enclosure at the "Ave Maria"
—or my ill-natured complaints. And yet she was so
generous, so queenly when there was a question of the
Order or of something to be done for the glory of God.
Splendid were her provisions for the chapel—*"Date et
dabitur."* She was like a queen decking the throne of
the King.

I remember saying, in one of our journeys when

we were guests of a splendid convent: "Oh! Mother!
I am so tired of poverty. When shall we taste a little
prosperity." She seemed deeply pained by the remark,
and begged me to take back the wish so contrary to
holy poverty and perfection, returning to the subject
again and again. And oh! how grinding poverty was
on our journeys. I climbed once the hill of Four-
vière with our little Indian girl, to obtain Our Lady's
help, for Mother was confined to bed, an empty purse
under her pillow. I remember the anguish of my heart
and mind that day. But Mother was saying the fifteen
mysteries whilst we climbed the hill, and when we returned to her the mail had come bringing our fare
home.

Our Lord always thus multiplied the loaves and
fishes when we had suffered enough, trusted enough.

Immediately after her Confirmation by Bishop
Rappe in Cleveland, Mother Amadeus began with her
school-girl friend, Mother Annunciation, a career of
penance. This she practised till death. *"O mulier inef-
fabilium."*

Corrosive sublimate, administered instead of salts
was another cause of crucifixion: constant ill-health,
fearful sleeplessness. I have spent nights endeavoring
to soothe her pain, whilst she lay motionless, her eyes
wide open till two and three in the morning; then she
would be up with the nuns at five to kneel erect during
Mass and morning meditation. "My favorite penance,"
she would say with St. John Berchmans, "is the common life."

Then on October 4, 1902, came the terrible railroad
accident at Billings, Montana. She lay long in bed, and
for eighteen weeks weights were fastened to her in-

VERY REV. JAMES KENT STONE, C.P., THE NEWMAN OF AMERICA.

jured leg; then for a long while after she could neither stand nor take her crutch alone. Then came felons, heroically borne and lanced, and the torture of the flexing of the knee!

I have seen her eat one cold potato and drink a glass of water at her principal meal after a hard day, for she would never suffer delicacies to be prepared for her. Unselfishness was her characteristic all the way through —the worst for her—the best for us always. Never, never, no matter what her illness, would she consent to break the fast or abstinence prescribed by the Church or by the Rule. She loved best the penances prepared by the Hand of God.

During the Chapter she scrupulously kept all the Roman fasts and these were all "black fasts." She would start off to see the wonders of Rome with nothing but a cup of black coffee for breakfast. Her spirit rose then and shone through the frail, ethereal frame. I remember her surprise at me, for I was often tired and out of humor. Mother Amadeus never seemed to know weariness in the presence of Rome's great wonders. "Man lives not by bread alone."

Mother Amadeus gave corrections with wondrous skill. She crushed you sometimes, but when she saw the sweet light of humility in your eye, she lifted you up again to her trust and love. She was so like Our Lord. You knew she loved you to the end. Her hand upon your brow dispelled the fiercest temptation. She could draw the thorn out of every heart. In her travels she was condescension itself toward the relatives of her companions; of her own she never spoke though they had attained eminence, and she loved them tenderly.

At sixteen she had made the vow of Perpetual Chastity. It was on July 11th, a sacred anniversary.

How exquisite was the purity of her looks, her actions. Never a caress. Never a kiss, save on the occasions prescribed by Rule. Frequent Communion, actual, spiritual, this was her joy. "Humility," she often said, with our dear Bishop Brondel, "humility is the chastity of the mind."

Mother Amadeus was a child with Rev. Father Lieter, S.J., with Bishop Brondel, with the Jesuit Fathers Treca, Damiana, S.J., Eberschweiler, S.J., her spiritual directors. Most scrupulously observant was she also of the Rule and Constitutions. Indeed, for a whole year, she made a vow never to break a single point of Rule. She grieved when this vow was lifted and said that year had been the happiest of her life.

Where obedience was concerned Mother Amadeus was unflinching. She spared not your foolish feelings, —an Abraham she, immolating her Isaac. That is how she accomplished so much. She was an Ursuline teacher every inch, grieving that her office of Superior left her no leisure for study. She procured exceptional advantages for her nuns. The best professors came for Latin, Greek, music painting, etc. She herself taught higher mathematics, and oh, how clear she made everything. It was my privilege to ring the rising bell, and when I came to Mother Amadeus I used to find her up, stealing a little time for study, or reading her first book on our dear Alaska.

"Promishleniki" (forerunner) she used to whisper to me, with her dear finger to her lips, for Alaska was our goal. We have seen how she lifted up the schools

in Toledo and Youngstown. But her teachings in the
interior, the spiritual life: these were ineffable!

Mother Amadeus' first and greatest love was the
Most Blessed Sacrament. Her preparations for Holy
Communion, her thanksgivings were ecstatic. The Holy
Gospel shows us Our Lord eternally persecuted. She
seemed to see this in the Most Blessed Sacrament, and
used to kneel erect and draw thence light and strength
for her manifold duties. "Rejoice, my child," she said to
me one day in an hour of great grief, "rejoice, because
if we are suffering it is because we love the Most Blessed
Sacrament."

She loved her Missal, the rites and ceremonies of
the Church, the office, Rogation Day, and Corpus Christi
Processions. At St. Peter's, before she became a
cripple, she decked the altars herself, and had wagon
loads of pine tree branches brought in from the mountains, which she herself planted to make an avenue
leading from the Church to the Convent. How eagerly
she presided when the novices were learning the Little
Office and the singing of the Tenebrae.

She loved the cloistered contemplative life. This
she told me at Cumberland, Maryland, in 1893 and at
Paray-le-Monial, 1901. Her love for the Missions, however, struggled with this hungry longing for penance,
enclosure and silent contemplation of the Most Blessed
Sacrament. I noticed that the contemplative nuns we
visited always clung to Mother as though she were their
own. There is no use trying to hide great sanctity. It
is a delicate perfume that pervades the atmosphere in
which you move. It steals away from you, unnoticed
by yourself alone.

Mother Amadeus said to me one day in June, 1903,

with the greatest candor and humility, that one of the
nuns thought she sought too eagerly the success of our
work. She asked me whether I thought her guilty of
so grave a fault. These lines are my answer. Dear
Mother never suspected that I was taking notes. But
I said to her that what had won me, and many others,
was the very reverse. She feared, she said, if an undertaking failed that failure was due to her sins or to her
lack of energy, that therefore she suffered most cruelly
by failure and strained every nerve, supernaturally, to
achieve success. I know of what I write, for when we
were in Italy sometimes this humble religious, when
there was no English speaking confessor available,
would ask her poor child for translations too sacred
and lofty for word of mine. Her own examinations of
conscience were perpetual, soul-searching, unflinching.
Are there spots on the sun?

Mother Amadeus never accepted a house without
stipulation for the Presence of the Most Blessed Sacrament. To live without Him was the only sacrifice she
would never make or ask of us. She asked me often
how I spent my time before the Most Blessed Sacrament,
and she never felt satisfied, never felt that I had been
there long enough. She loved to gather the Indian and
Eskimo children about her in chapel to pray aloud with
them, and they used to steal in and kneel beside her in
chapel and I with them, for she seemed to breathe Our
Lord's greeting, "Peace be with you."

The twentieth century has been called the century
of the "Adorers of the Most Blessed Sacrament."
Mother Amadeus of the Heart of Jesus was one of them.
I remember the joy at St. Peter's Mission when Mrs.
Mann of Washington sent us our first Ostensorium.

She fondled it, caressed it again and again. At our first Chapter General she pleaded that a daily visit to the Most Blessed Sacrament be made a point of Rule. Her dignity when she went and came from Holy Communion was marked. Her genuflection was concentrated love, something to be remembered, and this love for the Most Blessed Sacrament was translated in great love for the Sacred Heart of Jesus, great zeal in promoting the Devotion.

Baunard in his Life of the Blessed Mother Barat says that the characteristics of the saints of our day is their love for the centre of all truth—the Holy See, and their love for the centre of all charity, the Sacred Heart of Jesus.

The Blessed Virgin occupied the next place in Mother Amadeus' heart. It always took her an hour to say the rosary, but she never said it without a speedy answer from her "Mother." Then came St. Joseph, the Patrons of the Order and the "Little Flower of Jesus."

At Paray-le-Monial, Mother Amadeus prayed one afternoon from one to five, scarcely stirring; then she rose, greatly comforted, and with that far-away look that showed us how far above us she was, how much closer to God than were we. Upon this scene of a life, consecrated to love and to labor—a life too beautiful for mortal pen, let me lay down mine by tracing for you these last sacred words among Mother's papers after her holy death—the very few the great fire at St. Michael did not reach,—some of her resolutions during retreats. This sketch will have told whether she was faithful to them.

Subject of Particular Examen—Patience.
Never to let the least mark of impatience appear,

but on the contrary, *in all our words,* in all our *actions* and in our *countenance* to *show signs* of *great tranquillity* and *peace* of mind; and suppress all such motions as are opposite thereto. Sacred Heart of Jesus, make me patient.

Resolutions of the Retreat. To pass each day, night and hour of the year, August 1, 1900, August 1, 1901, as though it were to be the last year of my stewardship, my office, the *last year* of my life. Do each action in preparation for these ends. Get ready thy house and the house of thy soul for now is an account required of thee. I place this resolution under the protection of my dear Mother, the Blessed Virgin. Mary help me. I elect the Third Class ticket to Heaven. *"Domine, pati et contemnari pro Te."* Prefer the lowest rather than the highest, the poorest to the best, suffering to comforts, *unknown* to be known, common to uncommon, cheap to rich (personally), hard to soft, labor to ease, dishonor to honor.

St. Joseph, oh, lead me into the *hidden life.* Obtain for me great earnestness in learning the secrets of the Hidden Life, Mortification, throw away the body and great love of poverty practically. *Love* only the Blessed Sacrament. Do not try to gain the affection of any one for yourself. *Live* only by your spiritual exercises. Overcome false bashfulness in the performance of duty.

Mary Help! 1. Devote the next ten days from June 12th to June 22d to the Holy Spirit. Love the Blessed Spirit. Do your utmost to entertain Him in your heart. Try hard. Be faithful. Do not grieve Him by the least negligence. Ask the Blessed Virgin to make you understand. 2. The special resolution of this retreat is charity, especially not a word against charity to anyone especially _____. Not a word of fault-finding no matter *what happens.* If possible be patient. 3. Lecture, extra meditation in the afternoon, spiritual reading, so that your day may be according to the Rule. 4. Do not offend the Holy Ghost by negligence. 5. Do not lose your time.

Sum up.

1. The Holy Ghost—not to pain Him.
2. Charity.
3. Patience.
4. Spiritual exercises complete.
5. Not to lose time. Turn every minute to the Sacred Heart.
6. Good meditations that I may be a true lover of God, a true religious, a true Ursuline.

May we, dear Sisters, beloved friends, and benefactors meet some day in Heaven the great Mother Amadeus of the Heart of Jesus. I leave you, as her last legacy, the prayer that was on her lips always in hours of pain—pain both physical and moral:

"May the most high, the most holy, the most just will of God be done! May it be forever praised and glorified."

May this prayer strengthen and soothe you, too.